To: Daddy/Papa:

Happy birthday! We thought you'd enjoy reading about Hockey players + their family's.

love you forever,

Susan, Dave, Jennifer + Scott + Teddy
xo   xo   xo   xo

Hockey Dynasties

Hockey

Lance Hornby

Jack Batten

George Johnson

Bob Duff

Steve Milton

Dynasties

BLUE LINES AND BLOODLINES

Foreword by

Gordie and Colleen Howe

Mr. and Mrs. Hockey™

KEY PORTER BOOKS

Photo Credits

Hockey Hall of Fame: 16, 17 (Imperial Oil-Turofsky), 31
(top), 31 (lower) (Imperial Oil-Turofsky), 32 (Frank Prazak),
33 (Imperial Oil-Turofsky), 34 (Imperial Oil-Turofsky), 35
(Frank Prazak), 36-37 (London Life-Portnoy), 38 (Frank
Prazak), 47 (Imperial Oil-Turofsky), 48 (London Life-
Portnoy), 49 (O-Pee-Chee), 51 (Imperial Oil-Turofsky), 52
(Imperial Oil-Turofsky), 54-55 (Graphic Artists), 57 (Paul
Bereswill), 58 (Miles Nadal), 61 (Doug MacLellan), 62
(Paul Bereswill), 71 (O-Pee-Chee), 72 (Frank Prazak), 86
(O-Pee-Chee), 87 (O-Pee-Chee), 106 (Miles Nadal), 110-111
(Imperial Oil-Turofsky), 112 (Paul Bereswill), 115 (London
Life-Portnoy), 116 (London Life-Portnoy), 140 (Matthew
Manor), 141 (Dave Sandford), 142 (London Life-Portnoy),
143 (Miles Nadal), 152-153 (Imperial Oil-Turofsky, 165
(Graphic Artists), 166 (Paul Bereswill), 172-173 (Imperial
Oil-Turofsky), 174 (left) (London Life-Portnoy), 178
(Imperial Oil-Turofsky).

Bruce Bennett Studios: 21, 22 (lower), 23, 24, 25, 26, 27,
28-29, 30, 39 (lower), 40, 41, 42, 43, 44, 45, 46, 56, 59,
60, 63, 64-65, 66, 68-69, 70, 74, 75, 76, 77, 78, 79, 80,
81, 82, 83, 84, 90, 91, 92, 95, 96, 97, 98, 100-101, 102,
103, 104, 105, 108, 109, 113, 114, 118, 119, 120, 121, 122,
124, 125, 126, 127, 128, 129, 130, 131, 133, 134, 136, 138-139,
144, 145, 146, 147, 148, 149, 150, 151, 154, 155, 156, 157,
158, 159, 160, 161, 162, 163, 164, 167, 168, 169, 170, 171,
174 (right), 175, 177, 179, 180, 181, 182, 183, 184, 185, 186
(right), 187, 188, 189, 190-191, 192-193, 194, 196-197, 199,
200, 201, 202, 203, 204, 205, 206, 207, 208, 209, 210,
211, 212, 213, 214, 215, 216, 217, 218, 219, 220 (top), 221,
222, 223, 224, 225, 226.

Canadian Press Archives: 22 (top), 39 (top), 50, 89, 117,
123, 186 (left), 220 (lower).

National Library of Canada Cataloguing in Publication

Hockey dynasties : blue lines and bloodlines / foreword by Gordie and Colleen
Howe, Mr. and Mrs. Hockey ; general editor, Lance Hornby ; writers, Jack Batten
... [et al.].

Includes index.
ISBN 1-55263-464-7

1. Hockey players—Family relationships. 2. Hockey players—Biography. I.
Hornby, Lance II. Batten, Jack, 1932- III. Title.

GV848.5.A1H58 2002   796.962'092'2   C2002-903351-9

The publisher gratefully acknowledges the support of the
Canada Council for the Arts and the Ontario Arts Council
for its publishing program.

We acknowledge the financial support of the Government of Canada through the
Book Publishing Industry Development Program (BPIDP) for our publishing
activities.

Key Porter Books Limited
70 The Esplanade
Toronto, Ontario
Canada M5E 1R2

www.keyporter.com

Electronic formatting: Michael Callaghan

Printed and bound in Italy

02 03 04 05 06 6 5 4 3 2 1

To Dylan
AND THE NEW CENTURY
OF HOCKEY FAMILIES
L.H.

Contents

Foreword

ONE OF THE JOYS of the Howe family's long association with hockey is that we have never had to draw a line between our involvement in the sport and our family. Our hockey life and our family life always managed to fit together as if they were stitched by a master quilt maker.

Two seasons after I signed with the Detroit Red Wings in 1946, my younger brother Vic came from Saskatoon to play in Windsor—first for the Windsor Hettche in the International League, then for the Windsor Spitfires in the Ontario Hockey League. Having a brother across the Detroit River made it seem like I had brought my Saskatchewan roots with me.

Imagine how proud I was when Vic was called up to play for the New York Rangers in the 1950s. The first time we played against each other at Madison Square Garden, the team officials were against us having our picture taken together before the game. This was an era when you weren't supposed to talk to a player from another team. (I always thought that was kind of silly, and to be honest, I used to have Johnny Bower over to our house for dinner when the Toronto Maple Leafs were in town.) But by the time my brother arrived I was established as a player, and I essentially told them that family came first. We wanted that picture for our mom and dad back home. Nobody argued with me. Probably they knew I wouldn't back down on this issue.

What I remember is that Vic scored a goal against the Red Wings and I wanted to stand up on the bench and cheer. But I didn't. Later in that game I had a Rangers' player lined up to smack and I realized it was my brother and didn't follow through. It's funny what you remember. One of my Detroit teammates hit Vic hard and as I recall my head turned as if I wanted to get his number.

Looking back it was mostly confusing to play against my brother because family should always come first. It's difficult to reconcile your devotion to your family with your drive to win.

That's why it was more comfortable to play with our sons Marty and Mark on the Houston Aeros. There was no divided loyalty. If someone went after one of the boys, there was no confusion. In fact, I might have been a bit too aggressive for the sake of family loyalty. We still laugh about the time I jumped on a player who had attacked Mark; Mark told me later to be a little less aggressive because having my 205-pound frame on top of him caused the player more pain than the pummeling his opponent had inflicted upon him.

Colleen has never gotten enough credit for finding the loophole in the draft system that allowed the World Hockey Association to draft Mark as an 18-year-old and Marty as a 19-year-old.

The idea of us playing together was actually hatched at a March of Dimes Charity game in Detroit, where we were all on the ice. After that game, Colleen and I began talking about how nice it would have been if we could play together for real. That's when Colleen went to work studying draft rules. Not wanting to tip her hand, Colleen had her secretary call the WHA to see if it was following the same rules of only drafting 20-year-old players like the NHL. It was clear that the WHA officials hadn't even thought about that. Colleen then planted the seed by suggesting to Bill Dineen in Houston that the family could all sign with the Aeros.

When Houston picked Mark at the WHA draft in Winnipeg, there was quite a furor. But the WHA co-founder Gary Davidson ruled immediately that drafting Mark wasn't against any rules. The funny thing was that Bobby Hull immediately told a

10

Winnipeg Jets' official that he figured the entire Howe family would end up in Houston. He wanted the Winnipeg Jets to draft Gordie and then at least make Houston pay. But they didn't listen.

To get all of this organized was one of Colleen's greatest achievements, and she has had many others. In our first game with Houston, I was so nervous that my back went into spasms the night before. They had to hook me up to an electric heat machine between shifts to keep my muscles loose.

As everyone knows, we played quite well together in Houston. We won the Avco Cup in our first season with the Aeros. I won the MVP award and Mark was named Rookie of the Year. Also, we won again the next year.

Even though I won four Stanley Cup championships with the Red Wings, I still say playing with my sons was my greatest thrill. We have felt fortunate that our family life fit so well with our hockey life. All of our children feel blessed to have had the sport of hockey as their playground. Our son Murray even played on a junior team with Wayne Gretzky before deciding his calling was medicine. He is a doctor today in Ohio. We have now seen our grandkids play hockey. To the Howe clan, hockey has always been a family affair.

Gordie and Colleen Howe
Mr. and Mrs Hockey™

Lynn Gregg

Hockey Dynasties

The Hockey Family

In 1943, Reg, Max, and Doug Bentley suited up for the Chicago Blackhawks and became the first three brothers to play for the same team. While Doug and Max enjoyed successful careers, Reg was limited to just 11 games.

BILL BENTLEY was adamant.

He insisted that all six of his sons could have played in the National Hockey League, not just the two youngest.

Doug and Max combined to make four NHL first all-star teams in the 1940s, led the league in scoring three times, won a Hart Trophy and a Lady Byng, scored lifetime goals of 219 (Doug with the Chicago Blackhawks and New York Rangers) and 245 (Max with the Hawks, Toronto Maple Leafs, and Rangers), and played on three Stanley Cup champions (Max as a Maple Leaf).

But their father Bill insisted that Doug and Max's brothers possessed the talents to perform with the same magnificence in the NHL. It was mostly circumstances of a family nature that kept the older four close to their Saskatchewan homestead and out of the hockey limelight.

Bill was born in Yorkshire, England, in 1873, and grew up in Pembina, North Dakota, where he developed speed-skating skills at a nationally competitive level. In 1902 he made the trek north and west across the Canadian prairies, settling in Delisle, Saskatchewan (population: never more than 700).

Bill ran many business enterprises in Delisle, including gents' clothing and farm implements, but he kept a hand in wheat farming and raising cattle

and horses, which was where the home duties of the Bentley sons came into the picture.

Jack and Roy were the first two, both hockey stars in the Saskatchewan junior and senior leagues, but Bill anchored Jack and Roy in Delisle to tend to the cattle.

Wyatt, nicknamed Scoop, came next, and though he ventured far enough afield to play for Spokane in the Western Hockey League, his primary chore was to maintain the Bentley horses in racing trim. Next in seniority was Reggie, who managed a cup of coffee, or, in his case, a glass of beer, with Chicago in 1943.

On game days, rather than resting up in the afternoons like the other players, Reggie preferred to shoot pool and bend his elbow. With such a carefree attitude, he lasted just 11 games and one goal with Chicago before returning to the place where his father wanted him, working the family wheat spread in

Max and Doug Bentley worked hard and combined for a total of 464 goals in their Hall of Fame careers. Max scored 245 with the Blackhawks, Maple Leafs, and Rangers, while Doug netted 219 with the Blackhawks and Rangers.

Doug Bentley's pro hockey career spanned four decades.

Delisle and playing hockey for the nearby Saskatoon Quakers. With the older lads covering the necessary tasks on the home front, Doug and Max were free to dazzle fans and fellow players in the NHL.

As kids, Doug and Max prepared for their future careers by milking cows. This, Bill later figured, was how they developed the wrist power that gave the boys their characteristically wicked snapshots.

Both of them, small at no more than five-feet-eight and 155 pounds, possessed deft skills with the

puck; they were superb passers and stick handlers, something they acquired from two childhood sources. One was the non-stop summer games of ball hockey on the street outside their house, ten hours a day of Bentley boys with their sticks and a tennis ball. And the other was the oddly shaped rink that Bill Bentley flooded in the winter; a sheet of ice almost as long as an NHL surface but much more narrow, which put a premium on puck control and on a quick, darting mode of skating.

Max, the youngest of the Bentley boys, won both the Lady Byng and Hart Trophies during his career.

Equipped with such home-nurtured grounding in the hockey essentials, Doug and Max proceeded to NHL careers that culminated in Hockey Hall of Fame inductions (Doug in 1964, Max in 1966). But maybe, if Bill, the Bentley patriarch, had it right, there would have been a grand total of six Bentleys in the Hall.

In the long, astonishing, and honorable tradition of brothers at the highest levels of professional hockey —from Lester and Frank Patrick with the 1909–10 Renfrew Millionaires to six Sutter siblings with a collective 81 seasons in the past quarter century— the story of Doug and Max Bentley reflects a common experience. The factors that contributed to their hockey success were the same as those that marked the careers of the many brothers who have arrived

According to Bill Bentley, his sons Max and Doug *(shown here with Bill Mosienko)* were only two of his six sons capable of playing in the NHL.

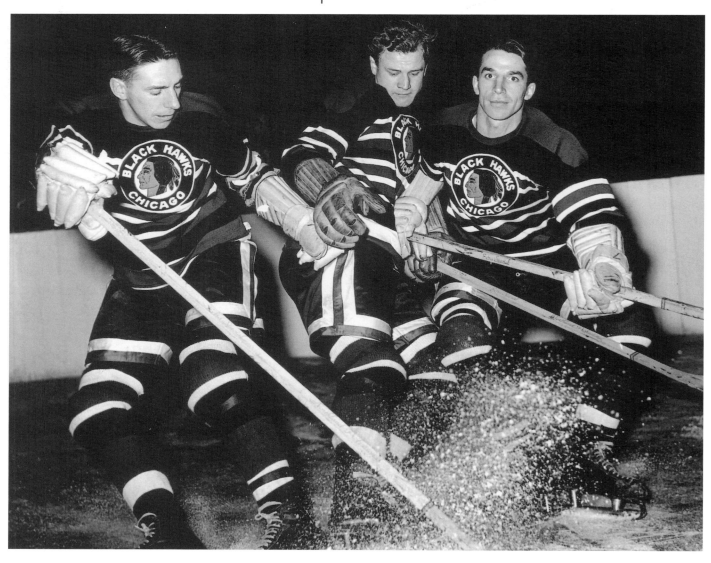

at the NHL in varying combinations and from widely differing backgrounds.

Genes, environment, a dash of good fortune, a share of familial support, and a measure of brotherly bonding . . . it's from these five elements that so many brothers like the Bentleys, and a surprising number of father-son duos, have emerged in such a demanding sport as hockey.

Genes? Doug and Max absorbed the skating inheritance from their dad, the youthful speed champ. And the right environment for hockey, of both the road and the ice variety, was as constant in Delisle as the prairie wind. As for the good fortune, it lay for Doug and Max in their ages, the last of the six boys and therefore the only two liberated to pursue the NHL.

It was also from the four older brothers, who mentored them as hockey kids and celebrated them as NHL stars, that Doug and Max derived the essential family support. The youngest two Bentleys bonded with all their brothers, but never as strongly as with one another.

They were also best companions on the ice until the November 1947 trade of Max from Chicago to Toronto that broke up the Hawks' dynamic Pony Line of Max at center, Doug on left wing, and the equally speedy Bill Mosienko on the right side. And Doug and Max remained each other's favorite and enduring company off the ice. They shared their accumulated hockey wisdom every day of their lives until November 24, 1972, when Doug died of cancer in Delisle, where he, Max, and all the other Bentleys made their permanent homes.

Genes are the most elusive of the five hockey elements. Just ask Vic and Vern Howe.

They were Gordie Howe's brothers, sons of the same parents, bearing the same genetic makeup and subject to the same influences. The boys' father

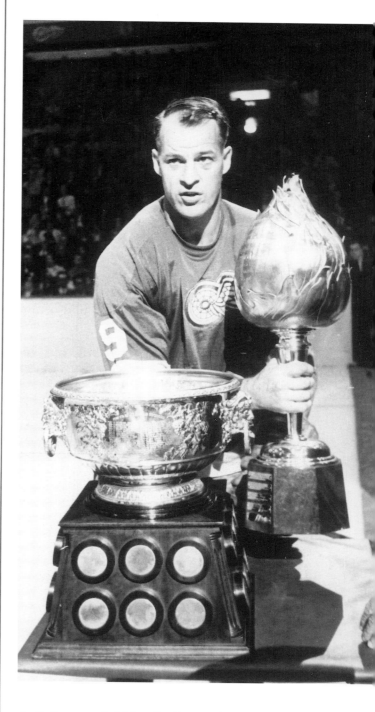

Gordie Howe won six Art Ross Trophies and six Hart Trophies during his illustrious 26-year NHL career, securing his place as one of the greatest players to strap on the blades.

worked at low-paying manual jobs for the city of Saskatoon, pouring cement for sidewalks, and handling the chores that called for muscle and heavy lifting.

The Howe family lived in a neighborhood where the houses had no hot water and where kids like Vic, Vern, and Gordie relied on the free baths provided by the local school. Life was hard for everyone, but one boy emerged as possibly the most accomplished of all hockey players while his two brothers made barely a dent in the game.

Gordie Howe scored 801 goals in the NHL, once considered a record for the ages; Wayne Gretzky surpassed the mark during the 1993-94 season.

Gordie played in an amazing 26 NHL seasons and scored 801 goals; Vic appeared in 33 games for the Rangers over three seasons in the early 1950s and scored three goals. Vern never reached the NHL.

The luck of the draw in genetics may explain only part of a hockey player's success. Joy in playing hockey, together with the pleasure of working zealously at the sport, accounts for a large share of the rest.

Gordie was the kid who loved to skate the full length of the slough that ran for four miles from the

Gordie Howe and Bobby Hull were two of the best players of their generation. Their sons would continue the tradition, going on to enjoy successful pro hockey careers.

edge of Saskatoon to the airport. He was the kid who spent the summers perfecting his powerful shot by driving a ball over and over into the side of the Howe house. And he put in the hours on the rink that a neighbor built in his backyard each year when the temperature fell below freezing.

The rink was not unlike the one that Bill Bentley flooded just down the highway in Delisle, fashioned in dimensions of 80 feet long

Gordie Howe was known by many names during his playing days. "Mr. Elbows" was one of them.

After an eight-year hiatus, Gordie Howe returned to the NHL with the Hartford Whalers for the 1979-80 season

Wayne and Brent Gretzky combined for 895 regular-season NHL goals—Wayne netted 894 of them.

by 30 feet wide. On this disproportionate surface, Gordie developed his phenomenal hand-eye coordination. He was having too much fun to realize it, but he was looking for hockey perfection. And he found it.

The Howe story raises another issue in hockey families: how does a younger brother, Vic in this case, cope with the problem of following an older brother who happens to be one of the best acts in the game? By the time Vic got to the Rangers in 1950, Gordie was already the star of the Cup champion Detroit Red Wings. The burden of expectation weighed heavily on Vic as he came into the game with the Howe name, and it ultimately proved too unfair a load.

It was Wayne Gretzky who best expressed the agony of pressure felt by Vic and by all of the younger brothers in hockey history. In the Gretzky family, Keith was five years younger than Wayne. At 12, Keith scored 115 goals, more than Wayne had potted at the same age. But the pressure of the Gretzky name soon overwhelmed Keith.

"If his name was Keith Smith, he'd be a rising star in an NHL organization," Wayne said astutely in 1990. "As it is, people are still asking him why he's not breaking my records."

Like Vern Howe, Keith Gretzky never played a game in the NHL. With considerably less buildup, Brent Gretzky, 11 years Wayne's junior, played 13 games for the Tampa Bay Lightning.

Brent Gretzky appeared in just 13 NHL games with the Tampa Bay Lightning, scoring one goal.

24

One player who bucked the name problem was Dennis Hull, younger brother of Bobby. Both Hulls, blessed with the same hockey genes, owe their strength and muscular dimensions to their father Robert, a lion of a man who worked for 47 grueling years in the Canada Cement plant near Eastern Ontario's Bay of Quinte.

Robert played senior hockey, and drove his kids to their hockey games and practices. Bobby flourished at an early age, and when Dennis, five years younger, proceeded along the same hockey path, he found it discouraging to face constant comparison.

"The newspaper coverage was always the same in junior A," Dennis says. "It would read, 'Bobby Hull's brother scored last night.'"

Bobby Hull, also known as the "Golden Jet," was feared for his speed and blistering shot.

But when Dennis joined Bobby with the Blackhawks in 1964, he realized the heat was off.

"I discovered that not only was Bobby better than me," Dennis says, "he was better than everyone."

Dennis Hull and brother Bobby played eight seasons together with the Chicago Blackhawks.

26

Lester Patrick *(pictured with sons Muzz and Lynn)* was a pioneer of the game, introducing the blue line, forward pass, and uniform numbers.

Dennis relaxed and enjoyed a superb 14-year career, scoring 303 goals and putting himself in position for a post-hockey life as a standup comic on the banquet circuit.

The Patricks made up the first and, as they are often described, the most "royal" of hockey families,

and it was their clan who established a pair of fundamental principles about the gene for hockey.

The first is that the gene can run astoundingly deep in generations, and the second is that the gene can work its impact on two aspects of the game, both playing and managing. Lester and Frank Patrick, born in 1883 and 1885, respectively, the sons of a well-to-do lumber baron, were pioneers in pro hockey. With Renfrew, they were the two of the highest-paid players in the sport—$3,000 per season for Lester, $2,000 for Frank.

In retirement, they founded the Pacific Coast Hockey League in 1911; built the first artificial ice rinks in Vancouver and Victoria, B.C.; and introduced such concepts as the blue line, the forward pass, and the fan-friendly notion of numbers on team uniforms.

Both Patricks hooked up with the management of NHL teams, Frank with the Boston Bruins and Lester in New York, where he served variously as the Rangers' coach and general manager for 20 years and won three Cups.

Lynn's sons, Craig and Glenn, put in 11 seasons of NHL play between them. Then Craig followed into coaching and management with the Rangers and the Pittsburgh Penguins.

In the matter of hockey environment, the second of the sport's five shaping elements, there seems to be nothing singular and definitive that produces the players of the NHL. The environment can be rural or urban, organized or free form, winter or summer, ice or street hockey, skates or sneakers.

It was the urban way with the Conacher clan. Three of them, Lionel, Charlie, and Roy, emerged from childhoods of shinny and pickup games in a working-class Toronto neighborhood to become stars at the very top of the NHL. Each was elected to first all-star teams (once on defense for Lionel in 1933–34, the same year that Charlie made the first

Craig Patrick's finest moment in hockey may have been winning the Lester Patrick Award (named after his grandfather) for outstanding service to hockey in the United States.

(following page) The 1938-39 New York Rangers were coached by hockey icon Lester Patrick *(top row, fourth from left)* and featured his sons Lynn *(top row, far left)* and Muzz *(top row, third from right)*.

Born and raised in Toronto, Charlie Conacher won a Stanley Cup with the Maple Leafs in 1932.

of his three appearances at right wing, and once on left wing for Roy).

Charlie twice won the NHL scoring title, in 1934 and 1935, Roy once, although Roy's 226 goals totaled one more than Charlie's. The brothers combined for five Cups, two for Lionel in successive seasons with the Hawks and the Montreal Maroons, one for Charlie with the Leafs, and two for Roy with the Bruins.

The brothers—Lionel was eight years older than Charlie, who was seven years senior to Roy—grew

Roy Conacher scored 226 goals in the NHL-one more than brother Charlie.

up in a family of ten kids, children of a teamster father who earned $20 in a very good work week. Home on Davenport Road in midtown Toronto was humble and cramped, and the sons found relief and purpose on the two hockey rinks in the playground at nearby Jesse Ketchum Public School. Charlie was such a lousy skater as a little kid that the others stuck him in goal to keep him out of the way. But he applied himself with dedication and made himself, as a pro, the swiftest Conacher with the hardest shot.

Roy was the brother who seemed a natural at the game, masterful at finessing the puck into the net, but he needed persuading by his older brothers before he committed himself to a hockey career. Lionel was the all-round athlete, so versatile that hockey was actually his fourth-best sport after football, lacrosse, and baseball, all of which he played at the highest Canadian levels.

Lionel, the eldest of the Conacher brothers, was instrumental in the development of his hockey playing siblings – both on and off the ice.

Charlie, Bert, and Lionel were three of ten Conacher children. While Charlie and Lionel went on to Hall of Fame careers, Bert missed his opportunity when he lost an eye in a road hockey game.

Brian Conacher, son of Lionel, played in five seasons with
Toronto and Detroit, winning a Cup with the Maple Leafs in 1967.

(opposite) Charlie Conacher went on to coach younger brother
Roy with the Chicago Blackhawks in the late 1940s.

Walter "Babe" Pratt won the Hart Trophy with the Maple Leafs
in 1943-44

But for each of the three boys, whatever their individual gifts, hockey began on the rinks in the schoolyard.

"We didn't have a penny as kids," Charlie once said. "But we knew that hockey could bring us something better in life, and Jesse Ketchum was where we learned the game. It was a hell of a lot of fun on that ice, but I'd be lying if I didn't say the money that us Conachers hoped to make one day was big motivation."

For many sibling players, the specific environment in which they are introduced to hockey influences the type of players they become. The two Hillman brothers, Larry and Wayne, and the three Plagers, Barclay, Bill, and Bob, flourished as hard-nosed NHL defensemen, a circumstance that wasn't unrelated to their hard-nosed hometown of Kirkland Lake in Northern Ontario.

Larry Hillman won Stanley Cups with Toronto, Detroit, and
Montreal during a pro career that lasted more than 20 years.

(following page) Babe's son, Tracy Pratt,
played 580 NHL games with six teams.

Wayne Hillman was a stay-at-home defenseman much like
brother Larry, one year his senior.

The same went for the Sutters, Brian, Brent,
Darryl, Duane, and twins Ron and Rich, who were
the products of the raw country around the town of
Viking, Alberta, where everyone, most notably the
Sutters, learned never to take a backward step on or
off the ice. They were all tough guys off the ice. In
these cases and many others, brothers moved to
forge their games in tune with one another and with
their mutual hockey surroundings.

Good fortune is underrated as a contributor to
family success, though not by the Lindros brothers,
who received theirs in mixed doses.

Eric has survived his terrible string of on-ice
concussions long enough to construct an all-star
career, while younger brother Brett, a player of
possibly equal promise, saw concussions limit him
to a mere 51 games in two seasons with the New
York Islanders.

On a significantly reduced scale, the Courtnall
boys, Geoff and Russ, suffered the same duality in
fortune. Russ, younger by three years, retired from
hockey by his own choice after 16 seasons and 297

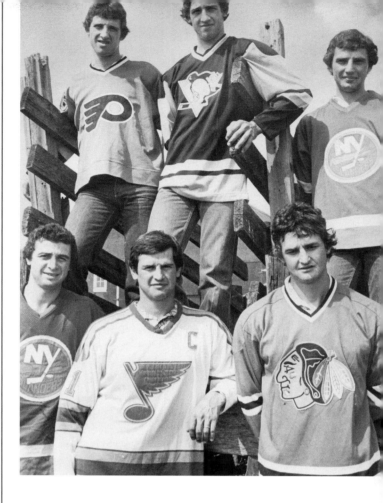

The Sutter brothers Ron, Rich, and Brent *(top row)* Duane, Brian,
and Darryl *(bottom row)* played in the NHL for a collective total
of 81 seasons.

Concussion problems ended the career of Brett Lindros *(right)*
and have threatened the future of brother Eric.

goals. But Geoff stretched his career for a few more valuable years until, like Brett Lindros, he became a concussion victim in 1999 and, much against his will, after 17 seasons and 367 goals, retired.

Perhaps the most heartbreaking victim of the quirks of hockey fortune was Bert Conacher, twin brother of Roy. As an adolescent, Bert showed the same dazzle on the rinks at Jesse Ketchum as his brothers. But his future was snatched away in a fateful game of street hockey in 1932.

Charlie was playing in the game; even though he was by then an NHL star with the Leafs, he still included himself in the family's ferocious road contests with sticks, a sponge ball, and empty coal sacks for the goalies' nets. Charlie and Bert were skirmishing for the ball when Charlie's stick flew up and accidentally cut Bert close to his left eye.

The game continued, Bert was stitched up, and nothing more was thought of the incident until eight months later, when Bert's vision faded. Charlie's stick had apparently nicked an optic nerve, and Bert went blind.

He was just 16, and though he continued to play junior hockey and to compete in the family pickup games, a career as an NHL star, which seemed as certain as the careers of his brothers, was forever denied.

Another kind of misfortune of a less-lethal variety has struck other sets of hockey brothers. This is the kind where one sibling receives the rewards and kudos, including Hall of Fame recognition, while the other, almost always of equal talent, finds himself unfairly overlooked.

Bill and Bun Cook *(flanking Frank Boucher)* **played ten seasons together for the New York Rangers.**

Drafted ninth overall by the New York Islanders in 1994, Eric Lindros's brother Brett was forced into retirement early in the 1995-96 season by a head injury. He was only 21.

Bun Cook amassed 158 goals and 302 points in 473 NHL games.

Bill Cook scored 229 goals in 475 games, all with the Rangers.

It was that way with Bill and Bun Cook. Bill, the eldest, had the flashier credentials. In 11 years with the Rangers, playing right wing on a line with Bun on the left side and Frank Boucher at center, Bill scored 229 goals, was a three-time first team all-star, and won induction to the Hall in 1952. Another brother, Bud, played 50 games between 1931–35.

On paper, Bun (given name, Frederick Joseph) appeared to have experienced a lesser career with 71 fewer goals in 11 years and no all-star honors. But Bun played a highly inventive brand of the game. He is universally credited with first conceiving the drop pass, while Rangers' teammate Alex Shibicky always claimed that Bun invented the slap shot. With all of these achievements, Bun was not elected to the Hall of Fame until 1995, 43 years after his brother.

As an illustration of tough love, Vladimir Bure stressed to his sons the need to settle for nothing less than the best personal results. Vladimir understood the pain of feeling second best. As a swimmer who specialized in freestyle events, he represented Russia at three different Olympic Games, in 1968, 1972, and 1976, and won four medals, a silver and three bronze.

Brothers Pavel and Valeri Bure won Olympic silver medals with Russia in 1998.

Valeri Bure was a second-round selection of the Montreal Canadiens in 1992, the year after his brother Pavel burst onto the NHL scene.

But Vladimir suffered the major misfortune of coming up against the greatest freestyle swimmer of the day, American Mark Spitz. At the 1972 Games, when Vladimir was at his peak, Spitz won seven gold medals. Vladimir loathed the defeats he endured, and when his two sons, Pavel and Valeri, began to emerge as two of Russia's finer hockey players, Vladimir filled them with competitive fire and preached that second is no good.

Under his father's prodding, Pavel emerged in the 1990s as a premier scorer, and Valeri, three years younger, has shown similar spectacular potential.

Pavel Bure is one of the most dangerous players in the league. He has twice scored 60 goals and has netted at least 50 five times.

From hockey's earliest days, fathers, not to mention older brothers and mothers, have found different ways to influence the hockey directions of their families' young players. Bill Cleghorn made such an impression on his sons, Sprague and Odie, that the pair turned into two of the toughest, meanest, most ornery players in the entire history of pro hockey.

The Cleghorns were a Montreal family, and Bill himself played an aggressive brand of lacrosse that earned him the macho nickname of Big Horse. His two sons, Sprague, born in 1890, and Odie in 1891, took up hockey, and Bill instilled in them his own take-no-prisoners approach.

An off-season trade in 2001 united the Bure brothers in Florida. The experiment was short-lived, however, as Pavel was moved to the New York Rangers midway through the 2001-02 campaign.

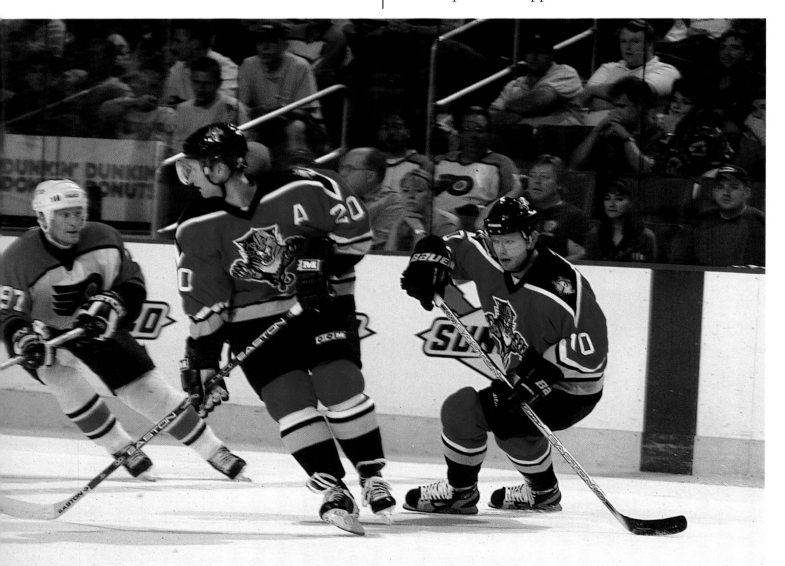

Bill was so single-minded on his kids' behalf that at least twice when he figured his sons needed support on the ice, he leaped over the boards in his galoshes and whacked the other teams' players with his cane.

It was small wonder that Sprague, especially, and Odie turned out to be hard cases in their hockey careers, which included ten NHL seasons.

In one 1922 game that lives in hockey infamy, the two brothers, teammates at the time with the Canadiens, knocked three star players of the rival Ottawa Senators out of commission: Eddie Gerard with a smack over the eye, Cy Denneny with a butt-end to the forehead, and Frank Nighbor with a charge.

"A disgrace to hockey," the game's referee, Lou Marsh, said later of the Cleghorns.

But "disgraceful" wasn't the only adjective that applied to the two. Sprague, primarily a defenseman, was slick as well as tough, and ended his career in the Hall. Odie, no slouch either, scored 95 NHL goals, helped to win one Cup (with the Canadiens in 1923–4) and was hired as the first coach of the Pittsburgh Pirates when the team entered the NHL in 1925–6. The Cleghorns were close, so close that Odie died two days after Sprague in July of 1956.

One irony in the workings of family support is that successful NHL players rarely exert much direct impact on their sons' approach to the game. Cal Gardner was one representative NHLer who was conscientious about deflecting from himself praise for the accomplishments of his two NHL sons.

Cal, a center in the 1940s and 1950s, played a dozen all-purpose years for four teams including two Toronto Cup winners. He could score a little (154 career goals), check a lot, play heads-up hockey, and go at an opponent with his dukes when needed.

Cal Gardner played nearly 700 NHL games and won two Stanley Cups with the Leafs.

Cal's two sons, Dave and Paul, created strong careers for themselves. Dave, the elder, put in seven seasons with five NHL teams and scored 75 goals; the fluid Paul had 402 points in ten seasons. But Cal always insisted that he had little to do with their success.

"All I gave them was the love and the support and maybe the right blood that runs in hockey families," said Cal, who died in 2001.

A former first-round pick of the Montreal Canadiens, Dave Gardner played 350 NHL games with five teams.

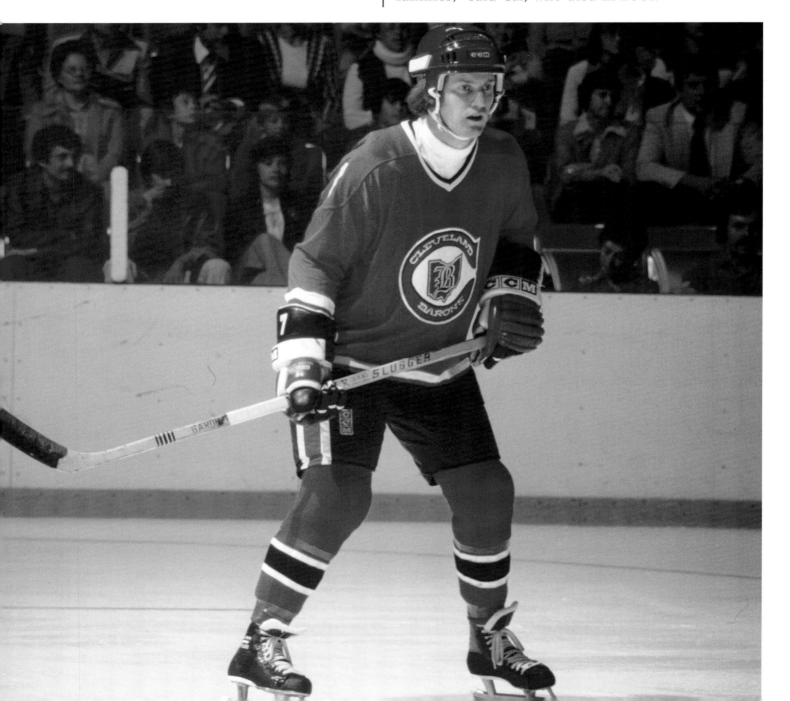

Cal's point was that, on weekends when Dave and Paul were engaged in kids' hockey in Toronto, he was busy himself, either playing or as color commentator on CKFH radio broadcasts of Leaf games.

"And besides," Cal said, "the thing is most former players are smart enough to realize that their kids can learn best from their own team coaches."

So it was that Dave came into hockey maturity under junior A coaching with the Toronto Marlboros, while Paul developed with the Oshawa Generals.

Four years younger than brother Dave, Paul Gardner resurfaced in the American Hockey League in 1996–ten years after retiring from the NHL.

Henri Richard (seated beside statue of brother Maurice) won a record 11 Stanley Cups with the Canadiens and was elected to the Hall of Fame in 1979.

Maurice and Henri Richard were 15 years apart in age but played together in Montreal for five seasons.

"Even before junior hockey," Cal added, "the person who deserved the credit for the way the boys turned out, the one who got them to games and practices, the one who was always there with the encouragement, wasn't me. It was the person who's overlooked in every hockey family—the wife and mother [Mary Gardner]."

Bonding, the fifth hockey element, is a sometime thing among the sport's brothers. Maurice and Henri Richard, arguably the most gifted pair of siblings in the game's history, never achieved bonding, though the personal distance between the two hardly prevented them from reaching greatness on the ice.

It was age that seemed to make the initial difference in the lack of Richard interaction, Rocket being so senior to Henri that he was out of their parents' family home, married, and a Canadiens' right winger before Henri turned seven. Thus the two shared little beyond the same background of childhood poverty in the Bordeaux neighborhood of north Montreal.

They were unalike in hockey styles and in their approaches to the world away from the sport. Rocket, the combustible star burdened by the adoration of Quebec fans, settled into a restricted post-hockey career as a Habs' glad-hander. Henri, unflappable and canny, grew financially comfortable from such enterprises as the Montreal tavern he ran for 26 years.

Maurice and Henri: same last name, same blood, but so opposite in life view that, in the five years during which their careers overlapped, they never sat together on the Canadiens' team bus or train or plane.

By contrast, the more inspirational bonding of the three Ottawa-born Cullen brothers, an element that helped immeasurably in fostering their hockey careers, has persisted long after they departed the NHL.

Brian is the eldest of the three, two years older than Barry and eight years senior to Ray. When Brian and Barry played together on the St. Catharines Tee-Pees, winners of the Memorial Cup in 1954, Bobby Baun was on the rival Marlboros. Years later, as Baun looked back on their mutual period in junior hockey, he characterized the Cullens as "the Gretzkys of their time."

Brian and Barry didn't operate at a Gretzky-like pace in the NHL, but both put in solid careers, Brian for seven years with the Leafs and Rangers, Barry for five seasons with Toronto and Detroit. Ray came along slightly later,

Brian was the eldest of the three Cullen brothers. Bobby Baun characterized the trio as "the Gretzkys of their time."

SYL APPS
WALTER BRODA
GORDON DRILLON
TIM DALY

P.	W.	L.	T.	FOR	AG.	PTS.
48	22	21	5	119	115	49

FINNIGAN
NICK METZ
BOB DAVIDSON
ART JACKSON
JACK SHILL
TIM DALY

P.	W.	L.	T.	FOR	AG.	PTS.
48	23	19	6	126	106	52

beginning his NHL career after his older brothers had left the league, and scored 92 goals in six strong seasons.

But what became more essential to the brothers in the long run was their close relationship and a plan for the family beyond hockey.

Brian set the plan in motion during his years with the Leafs. He became acquainted with a hockey fan named Herb Kearney who owned the Hearn Pontiac-Buick dealership in Toronto's west end. Brian worked part-time at Hearn through his Leaf tenure, and when he retired in 1963, he joined Hearn's leasing division.

Four years later, leaning on his hockey friendships for promotion help, Brian opened his own Pontiac-Buick dealership in St. Catharines. Barry followed Brian and Ray followed Barry into the business.

Today, all three brothers are proprietors of their own dealerships across Southern Ontario. It's a life that began in hockey bonding and has continued into a second generation through Barry's son John who played splendidly with four teams over 11 seasons.

Non-Hodgkins Lymphoma struck John in 1997, and forced him from the game; and though he made it back to play briefly, he retired for good in 1998–99. But now, with the cancer in remission, John is reworking his life in cars with Terry Cullen in an Atlanta dealership owned by his non-NHL brother.

The Cullens have carried the process significantly beyond the Patricks' story. Brian, Barry, and Ray have demonstrated that hockey brothers can both flourish within the sport and translate the lessons learned in its arenas—dedication, accountability, comfort in the public eye—to prosper in the world outside the sport.

Barry Cullen *(shown with Bob Pulford)* played with brother Brian in Toronto for three years. His son John went on to play over 600 games in the NHL.

(following page) Ray Cullen scored a respectable 92 goals playing parts of six seasons with the Rangers, Detroit, Minnesota and Vancouver.

The Dynasties

2

A successful career coupled with his passion for the game led Brian Sutter behind the bench soon after retiring in 1988. It turned out to be a good fit: he won the Jack Adams Trophy as coach of the year in 1990-91.

THE ONE-UPMANSHIP started with something as trivial as scrapping over the last homemade bun on the family dinner table Sunday nights.

"Oh, we fought about everything, competed for everything," recalls Brian Sutter. "Who could

carry out the heaviest pail of water. Who'd score the last goal before Mom called us in from the rink before bed. Who could spit the farthest. Who was the best arm wrestler, the best baseball pitcher, the best road hockey player. You name it, we felt like we had to beat each other at it."

Of hockey's brother-playing dynasties, none begins to approach the lore of the Sutter brood of Viking, Alberta. Oh, sure, maybe two siblings skating in the NHL at one time, on the odd occasion three. But six? Like Joe DiMaggio's 61-game hitting streak, Wilt Chamberlain's 100-point game, or Glenn Hall's 502 consecutive games played in goal, that record is safe. Probably for all time.

Arguably the most talented Sutter, Brent played over 1,100 games and won two Stanley Cups with the New York Islanders.

As a player, Brian Sutter combined grit and skill, scoring 46 goals and amassing 254 penalty minutes with the St. Louis Blues in the 1982-83 season.

"Sutter hockey" has come to represent many things to many people: Unflinching effort. Willingness to subjugate self for the many. Withering frankness.

Once, when coaching the Calgary Flames, Brian was asked about his relatively small lineup.

"It's not the size of the bull," he barked, "it's how well he's hung!"

In an age of hockey millionaires, they were old school in the very best sense of the term. At the core of the legend is an indomitable heart, a fierce—almost ruthless—desire to succeed and not to compromise themselves, their teammates, or their employers.

Sutters played hard. Sutters played hurt. Sutters played the hand they'd been dealt. When Darryl stepped aside as coach of the Chicago Blackhawks in 1995 to spend more time with son Christopher, born with Down's syndrome, everyone nodded. Why, of course he did the right thing, they murmured. He's a Sutter.

"There's nothing magical about it," protests Brent. "We never thought much about having six brothers in the NHL. First off, it was Brian's dream. When he made it, then it became Darryl's dream. And so on, down the line."

There hadn't been so many Canadian kids this famous come from one family since the Dionne Quintuplets. The tiny farming community of Viking, pop. 1,200, became renowned for turning out hockey players the way Detroit turns out cars or Italy turns out tenors.

The tales of the Sutters spending summers playing shinny in the hayloft are the stuff of Canadian legend; a country's equivalent of a young Cassius Clay having his bike stolen and learning how to box to make sure it never happened again.

An 11th-round draft pick of the Chicago Blackhawks in 1978, Darryl scored 40 goals for the team in 1980-81. Following brother Brian's lead, he went on to coach the Hawks and San Jose Sharks.

60

None of Grace and Louie's six NHL-playing offspring—Brian, the eldest; Brent, arguably the most innately talented; Duane; Darryl; and the twins, Rich and Ron—won a Hart, Art Ross, or Conn Smythe trophy. Nevertheless, they made a profound impact on the game.

Astonishingly, from 1976 through 2001, there was at least one Sutter playing in the NHL at any time. Together, they accounted for over 4,994 regular-season games, 1,300 goals, 2,900 points,

Brent Sutter played with the New York Islanders during the dynasty years of the early 1980s.

7,000 penalty minutes, and more elbows, stares, and cuss words than could be tallied by the most sophisticated computer.

"Do I like the Sutters?" Hall of Fame goalie Glenn Hall once asked. "Right down to the little sneer."

That so many of them remain involved in the game is a testament to both their passion for it and the remarkable niche they have carved.

Duane coached Florida for a spell. Brian is a former Jack Adams Award winner, and was a

Rich Sutter's career lasted 13 seasons and found him suiting up for seven different teams.

frontrunner in 2001–02 for resuscitating the Blackhawks. Darryl's San Jose Sharks are a viable Cup contender. Brent owns, manages, and coaches the Western Hockey League Red Deer Rebels, Memorial Cup champions in 2001. Both Rich and Ron are NHL scouts.

Ron was the last of the Sutters playing in the NHL. The grinder retired with the Flames after the 2001 season.

"Hockey," says Brian simply, "is all we ever wanted to do."

Brent never wears the Cup rings he owns, won with the New York Islanders in the early 1980s, nor the three he received for Canada Cup glory. Not because he isn't proud, but because what's ahead of a person is the important thing, not what's behind. Another Sutter code to live by.

"People always wonder how we all turned out so similar in our attitudes," says Brent. "Well, in my mind, there were two reasons: The discipline Mom and Dad instilled in us, and the fact there were so many of us. By discipline I mean getting off the school bus and knowing there were chores that had to be done around the farm. Not thinking of a way to get out of them or finding an excuse to put them off or whining about how unfair it was. Just doing them, whether that meant getting on the tractor out in the fields, feeding the cattle or the pigs, mending a fence. Whatever. If one of us wasn't around, someone else took on his work.

"And with so many of us in the family, well, we got used to a team atmosphere very quickly. You had to trust the brother next to you, the same way you have to trust the teammate next to you."

With six brothers playing in the NHL at once, there was plenty of occasion for Sutter vs. Sutter match-ups.

(following pages) Twins Rich and Ron Sutter played together for the Flyers in the mid 80s and the Blues in the early 90s.

On October 30, 1983, history was made when four brothers—Rich and Ron for the Philadelphia Flyers, Duane and Brent for the Islanders—met in the same game.

"Don't know why everyone made such a big deal when we'd play against each other," scoffs Brian. "Did it all the time growing up."

The most difficult Sutter to play against, even for a Sutter? Brent chooses the twins, partially

Many players felt the wrath of the Sutter brothers during their playing days.

because he grew up closer to them in age, and also because the Isles and Ron and Rich's Flyers, were arch-rivals.

"Duane," replies Brian. "They didn't call him Dawg for nothing. He was like a Dawg. Always barking at you and nipping at your heels. He was a real pain in the ass. He had something to say all of the time and said nothing most of the time. But he got his job done."

(following page) By the time Rich and Ron were eligible for the NHL draft, teams were wise to the value of having one of the Sutters on the roster. In the 1982 season, Ron was taken fourth overall by the Flyers and Rich, tenth overall by the Pittsburgh Penguins.

"Terrible" Ted Lindsay followed his father to the NHL and was instrumental in the creation of the NHLPA.

They all did.

Dynasties in hockey haven't been restricted to on-ice talent, however. Through the years, certain families became almost as famous for owning teams as the star players they paid, promoted, and often fought with.

First and foremost, the Norris family owned and operated the Detroit Red Wings for half a century, beginning in 1932 when grain millionaire James Norris bought the ailing franchise and immediately added the famed winged-wheel insignia, borrowed from a cycling club he belonged to in Montreal.

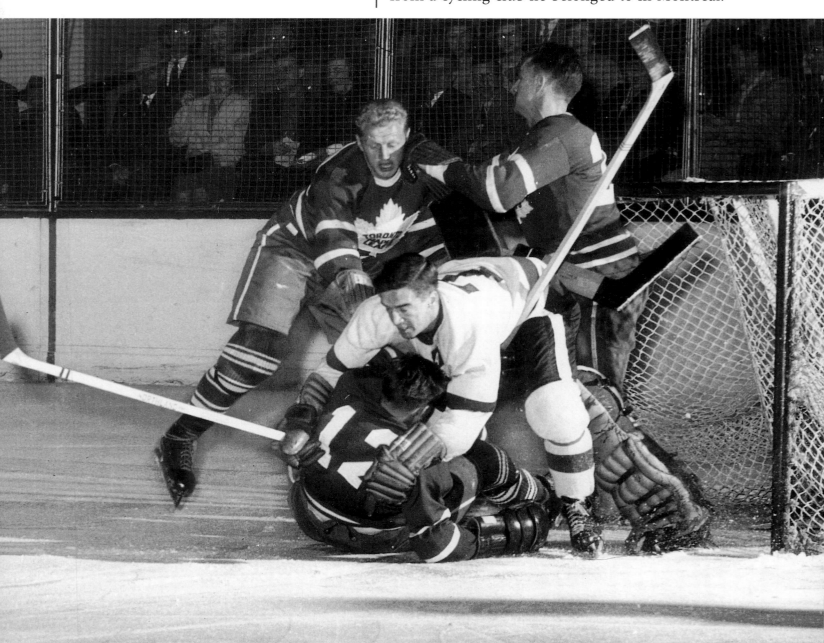

Under the Norris reign, the Wings would become the most successful U.S.-based franchise, winning seven Stanley Cups and showcasing the likes of Black Jack Stewart, Gordie Howe, Sid Abel, Ted Lindsay, Terry Sawchuk, Alex Delvecchio, Marcel Pronovost, and Red Kelly.

The Norris era ended when Detroit pizza baron Mike Illitch took control of the club in 1982, following a string of disappointing seasons.

"They just got rid of so much great talent," Howe reflected later. "They made bad trades, the people didn't come up through the system, and they made more bad trades trying to fill the holes."

In 1952, the Norris family and Arthur Wirtz joined forces to purchase the Blackhawks. Two years later, Arthur and brother Michael Wirtz gained controlling interest of the club, which eventually passed to Arthur's son, Bill.

Dubbed "Dollar Bill" by his critics, including countless Chicago fans, he's been accused of allowing talent such as Chris Chelios, Jeremy Roenick, and Eddie Belfour, among others, to leave over money issues. The fiscal squabbles go as far back as 1972, when superstar left winger Bobby Hull jumped ship and, with the stroke of a pen, legitimized the upstart World Hockey Association.

The Blackhawks haven't won the Stanley Cup since 1961, and have seen a fair share of controversy —and the ride has never been dull.

Among expansion franchises, none has enjoyed the ongoing prestige or success of the Flyers, which is largely due to the ownership of Ed Snider, a former football executive, and his family.

Starting in the 1967 expansion of NHL with just 2,100 season ticket holders, the Flyers grew to win two Cups during the infamous Broad Street Bully years and endured only five sub-.500 seasons in the past 30.

Jeremy Roenick was one of the high-profile players to leave the Chicago Blackhawks over money issues. Second-generation Blackhawk owner "Dollar" Bill Wirtz has been long criticized for his squabbles with top players.

Alex Delvecchio played 24 seasons for the Detroit Red Wings during the era of the Norris family. They owned the Red Wings for 50 years.

Tired of his dealings with Bill Wirtz, superstar Bobby Hull shocked everyone when he signed with the Winnipeg Jets of the World Hockey Association.

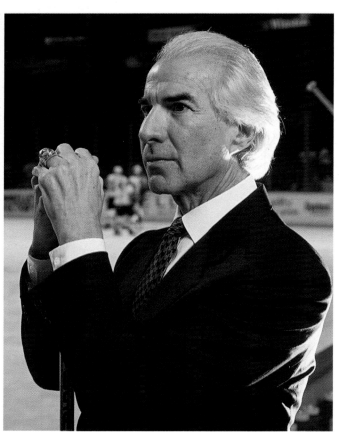

The Knox family—headed by Seymour III and Northrup—was responsible for bringing the NHL to Buffalo and owned the Sabres for 28 years, until the team was sold to John Rigas, founder and chief executive officer of Adelphia Communications Corp. Truth be known, when Seymour Knox died of cancer on May 22, 1996, a lot of the pioneering spirit and vision that was the Sabres went with him.

If there was a logical extension to the Sutter family's good western Canadian stock, it would be the Ontario-based Plagers.

"Fearless," says Scotty Bowman, the boys' coach at St. Louis, in tribute. "They were absolutely fearless."

Barclay, Bob, and Billy, all defensemen, grew up in a hockey culture where their dad, Gus, would referee his kids' games.

Ed Snider and his family are responsible for the initial and continued success of the Philadelphia Flyers.

Following the lead of the Bentleys, the Plager brothers skated together for the St. Louis Blues in the late 1960s and early 1970s.

"We never got a break," laughs Bob Plager, now a scout for the Blues. "We'd get home mad, be sitting around the kitchen table. Silence. Then one of us would start griping. 'That was a cheap penalty you called on me in the third period.' And Dad would pull out a rule book—he always seemed to have a rule book in his back pocket—and start thumbing through it.

"'Cheap penalty?' he'd say. 'Hmmm, I can find hooking and holding and tripping in here but no cheap penalty. Nope, no such thing as cheap penalty. But you say I called one on you? That's odd.'"

Barclay *(shown here on the receiving end of a Tiger Williams punch)* was the most physical of the hockey-playing Plagers. He finished his career with over 1,100 penalty minutes.

"They'd fight," recalls former teammate Terry Crisp. "Ooh, how they'd fight. But let anyone else get mixed up in it, and you'd have to deal with all three of them. All you had to say to Barc or Billy was 'You're right, Bobby's a jerk,' and they were all over you like a pack of wolves."

"I remember talking contract with Bob one time," reminisces Bowman. "In those years, players didn't have agents. They negotiated for themselves. So he comes into the office, sits down, looking for

Bob Plager moved behind the bench after his playing days and was awarded the 1990-91 IHL Commissioner's Trophy for coach of the year by his peers.

$20,000 or something like that, and says 'I know you'll be fair. Give me what you think I'm worth.'"

"Then he paused, and looked at me hard and said, 'But I'm not taking a penny less than my brother!'"

If elder brother Barclay was the soul of the trio and Billy, the youngest, the most laid-back, then Bob, one of the most feared hip-checkers of his era, could be best described as the clown prince.

Bob and Barclay Plager were defense partners during their days in St. Louis.

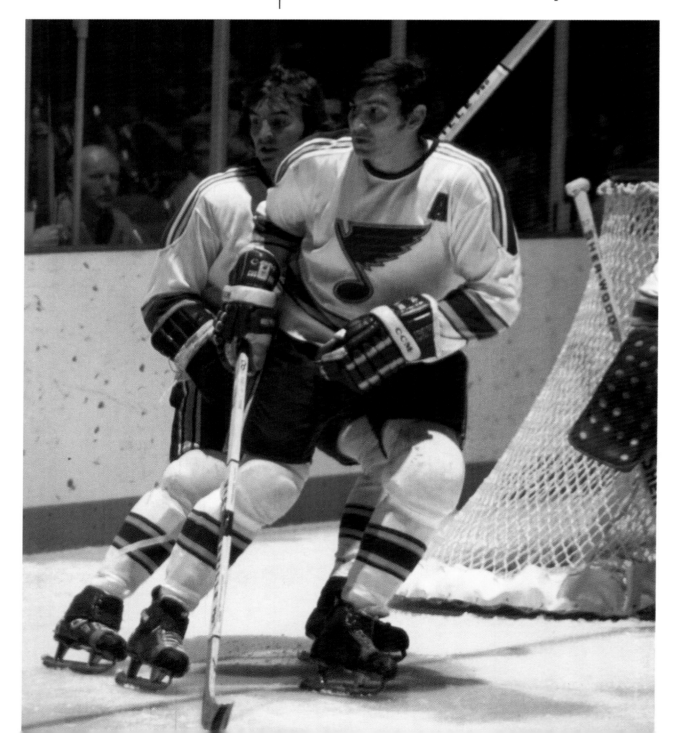

Early in his tenure as a Blue, Plager convinced writers in St. Louis that his mother, whom he called Big Ede—"Edith," says Crisp, "one of the sweetest women you'll ever meet"—was the women's professional wrestling champion of Canada and that he had made a few extra bucks during one stretch as a beer taster at a local brewery. The story was written up, then exposed.

"Some of those [writers]," cackles Crisp, "still aren't talking to Bobby."

"Bobby," recalls Glenn Hall, "would kid anyone. And he was merciless.

Bob Plager was a stay-at-home defenseman, scoring just 20 goals in 644 career games in the NHL.

"Billy had a speech impediment, couldn't say his Rs. So Bobby would be standing on the ice and say to Billy, 'Who's that No. 4 again?' (meaning Pittsburgh Penguins' Duane Rupp). And Billy would answer 'Duane Wupp.' And Bobby would say 'Duane who?' And Billy would answer 'Duane Wupp.' And Bobby would repeat 'Who?' And Billy, who was ready to explode by now, would be screaming 'Duane Wupp! Duane WUPP! DUANE WUPP!'"

Bob would go on to play 644 regular-season games, and 74 more in the playoffs as the expansion Blues advanced to Cup finals their first three seasons.

Billy, who now works for Quaker Oats in Kirkland Lake, played in 263 for the Blues, Minnesota North Stars, and Atlanta Flames.

Barclay Plager went on to coach the St. Louis Blues after retiring as a player.

The Plagers, everyone figured, were tough enough to take on anything. Turns out everyone was wrong. The family, the Blues, and the hockey community were stunned when Barclay the strong, Barclay the indestructible, was diagnosed with brain cancer in the late 1980s.

The eldest Plager battled it with the same ferocity he used against Bobby Hull, Phil Esposito, and Wayne Cashman. Plager kept up a brave face during treatments, even continuing to help coach the Blues for a time. He craved being around the game, around the rink.

In the end, all the effort, all the humor, all the tenacity in the world couldn't save Barclay, who passed away February 6, 1988.

In the end, says Brian Sutter, "Barc couldn't take the hell anymore. He'd suffered enough. In Canada, for some reason, we seem embarrassed to admit we have heroes. Well, Barc was a hero of mine. Of anyone who knew him."

"I have to believe," says Bob, "that he held on as long as he did because he knew all his friends were coming to St. Louis for all-star week that year and he wanted them to be there when he died. He waited for them and passed away two days before the game."

Bob says St. Louis has never forgotten Barclay.

"People will sometimes get the names mixed up and call me Barclay or ask if I was one of the Barclay brothers," Bob said. "Then they get kind of embarrassed, y'know, and start to apologize. I just

Sylvain Turgeon was the second overall pick in the 1983 entry draft. He went on to play 669 games during an injury-plagued career.

Pierre Turgeon did older brother Sylvain one better – he was taken first overall in 1987 and has gone on to post-Hall of Fame numbers with five NHL teams.

stop 'em dead in their tracks. I tell 'em, 'It's okay. In fact, I'm damn proud you think of me as one of the Barclay brothers. That's more than good enough for me.'"

If courage was a Plager family hallmark, the Stastnys from Bratislava could claim the same, although in a very different form.

Yes, it takes fortitude to drop in front of a 100-mph shot or lose your bridgework while chipping a puck out of the defensive zone late in a tight game. But leaving your homeland, your way of life, what you know—now that really takes chutzpah.

Peter, Anton, and Marian Stastny overcame incredible odds to skate together on the same line for the Quebec Nordiques for four seasons.

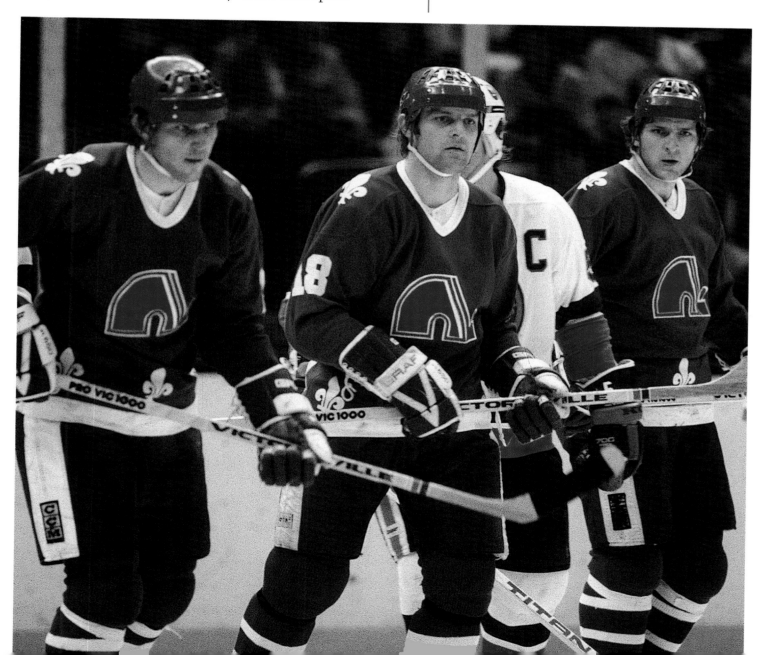

"Looking back, I wonder how we did it," admits Peter Stastny today. "We lived in a vicious, vicious system, where the authorities would take revenge to make sure no one else would follow in your footsteps. We worried about our parents, our friends.

"Eventually, though, they left us no choice. They were trying to take away what we loved for us, the game of hockey. I wouldn't stand for that. Anton wouldn't stand for that."

So Peter and Anton decided to defect, to escape the suffocating restrictions of the old communist Czechoslovakian regime. A husband and wife could travel together, but not an entire family. So older brother Marian, the father of three, decided to stay behind, at risk to himself and his family.

A precedent for smuggling a player out of an Iron Curtain country had been set when the WHA's Toronto Toros spirited Vaclav Nedomansky from Czechoslovakia in 1974. With angry Czech authorities on guard, prying the Stastnys free would require a good deal of planning. Initially, the brothers balked, recalled Quebec Nordiques owner Marcel Aubut.

"Each brother was not prepared to say 'forget the family and forget the house. Forget my popularity, forget my country, my nation, my language, all those things' and leave. They were not prepared to do it," Aubut said.

"But as they felt the oppression within the Czech system becoming more and more stifling, Quebec's entreaties looked better and better."

Team exec Gilles Leger masterminded the break-out, an Ian Fleming-esque bit of subterfuge that included a mysterious ally and friend of the Stastnys known forevermore as—yes—007, to drive Peter's pregnant wife Darnia to Vienna, while Leger and Aubut whisked Peter and Anton to join her.

Peter Stastny won the Calder Trophy as rookie of the year in 1981. He finished his career with 1,239 points, and in 1998 he was inducted into the Hockey Hall of Fame.

Once in Vienna, the brothers were hidden in a hotel room under Aubut's name until the Nordiques received safe passage for the brothers and Darnia from the Canadian embassy in Austria. On their way out of the country, however, they were spotted by Czech secret security and escaped by the skin of their teeth.

On August 25, 1980, Peter and Anton arrived in Canada, landing in Montreal. Their impact on the NHL, and the Nordiques in particular, would be profound. That first season, Peter, 24, tallied 109 points and won the Calder Trophy. But without the third member of their line, the brothers felt incomplete.

Getting Marian to North America to join them took the Nordiques an entire year to co-ordinate. He was under 24-hour surveillance by Czech authorities and, according to Peter, had lost all his friends because they would be interrogated following each visit.

"I was in Las Vegas with my wife and other NHL players when I heard Marian had arrived in Austria," Peter said. "It was the biggest relief of my life." Among hockey's family dynasties, the Stastnys are indisputably unique.

"To have three brothers together, on the same team, on the same line, I think is impossible again," says Peter, proudly. "And we had success because we had different strengths as players.

"Marian was dynamic, explosive, aggressive. A great release. I had the vision, the ability to make a pass. I was a born centerman. Anton had many of Marian's qualities, but when you're the youngest of three, you take the role that's left."

Which left him to go and get the puck to get to Peter to give to Marian.

"It is the joy, the highlight of my career, playing on a line with my brothers," Peter said. "We fit

Marian was the last of the Stastnys to come out from behind the Iron Curtain. He had 89 points as a 28-year-old rookie with the Nordiques.

Anton, the youngest of the Stastny brothers, averaged just under a point per game during his days in the NHL.

together so well. I only wish it could've lasted longer.

"What we all shared was a competitive spirit; a love of hockey. To play at the Olympics in Lake Placid together and the World Championships and then to be on the same line again in the NHL . . . I think it would be every boy's dream, don't you?"

Today, Peter scouts for the Blues and headed up the Slovakian team, which competed at the 2002 Winter Olympics and won the 2002 World Championships. Marian owns and runs a golf course in Quebec City. Anton moved back to Slovakia and is in charge of an import-export business.

Peter was as close to a complete player as could be found in the game. Intelligence. Flair. Stamina. Size. Desire. Consummate skill. He was blessed with the works. His seventh-game overtime goal to slay the arch-rival Canadiens in 1985 at the Forum, hockey's hallowed hall, remains a touchstone moment for Quebec City hockey fans to this day.

Peter would play 15 NHL seasons, piling up 450 goals and 1,239 regular-season points, while Anton lasted nine years and Marian five. In 1998, Peter was enshrined in the Hall of Fame.

"Playing in Quebec as he did, I don't know if people in other cities realized how good Peter was," says the Nords' coach at the time, Michel Bergeron. "But in Quebec everyone loved him; everyone knew he was a superstar. He learned French quickly and became a real part of the community.

"I'm not saying Marian and Anton weren't fine players. But on the ice, Peter was special."

Peter said the clandestine defection was worth the risk.

"As it turns out, our leaving did a lot of people good," says Peter. "Because we were so high profile, the authorities there were afraid to do anything; to exact any sort of revenge.

Peter Stastny represented Slovakia at the 1994 Olympics, 14 years after fleeing the country. He has gone on to become a major force in Slovakian hockey.

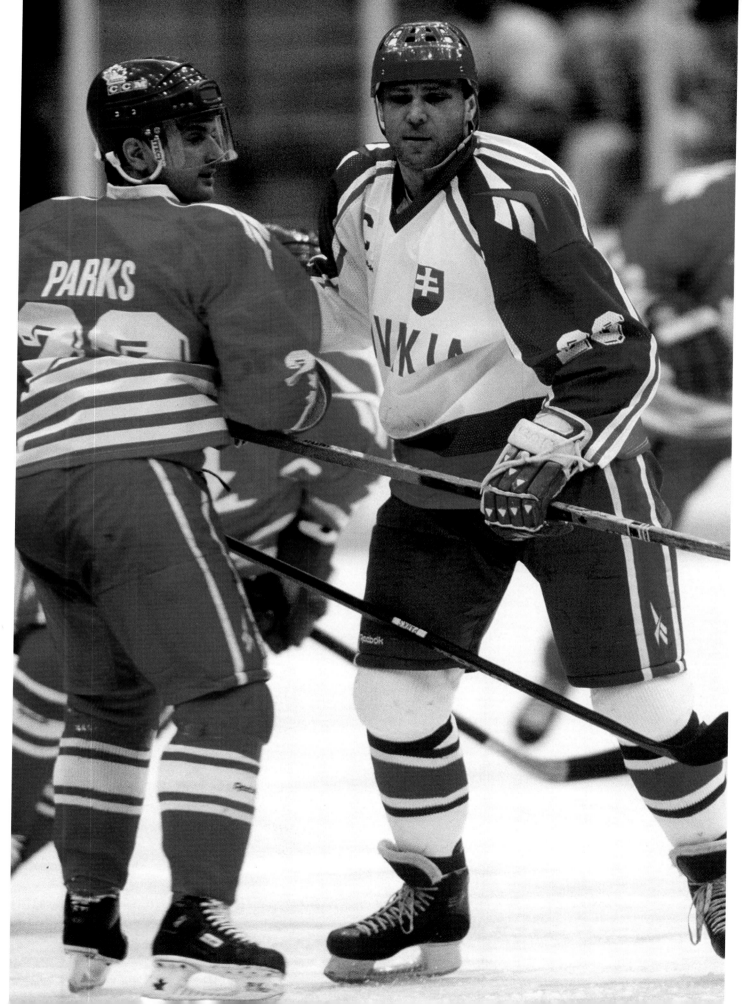

90

Dale Hunter had an outstanding NHL career, amassing over 1,000 points during his 20 years in the league.

"I like to think people believe we were good players, and that we were strong enough to stand up for what we believed in."

The Hunter brothers of Petrolia, a hardscrabble oil and gas town located in southwestern Ontario, stood up and were counted in their own way, too.

"Today, kids get home and they plop down in front of the TV or the Nintendo or the computer," says Mark Hunter. "Us, we had responsibilities on the farm, responsibilities to help the family out.

"Oh, there's no question that mindset helped the three of us make it to the NHL. It's helped us through our whole lives, actually. Farming, hockey, business, they're all a question of rolling up your sleeves and getting down to work."

And the worst job on the farm?

"Oh, I hated shovelling the muck behind the cattle. Not exactly your A-1 job. It's bad enough having to shovel it without having a cow trying to kick you in the head."

They were born two years apart, Dave in 1958, Dale in 1960, and Mark in 1962. Dave turned out to be the checker of the trio, considered so valuable a property by general manager Glen Sather among a gaggle of superstars in Edmonton.

Mark was the sniper and Dale the rabble-rouser and consummate team leader. Another brother, Ron, reached the junior A level.

During the boys' formative years, their dad would deliver them to the local rink. But with the farm's operation at stake due to their absence, he told them that there would no slacking off on the ice. Have fun, but don't keep anything in reserve. Otherwise, you're just wasting everyone's time.

Like the Sutters, blood ties in the Hunter household had to be sacrificed momentarily in favor of team ties. The seething hatred between Mark's

Mark, the youngest of the Petrolia, Ontario-born Hunter brothers played 13 years in the NHL.

Canadiens and Dale's Nordiques put them in constant conflict.

During a memorable major melee back in 1983, Mark, seeing Dale with a clear advantage over teammate Mario Tremblay, jumped his brother, and the photo of the two of them rolling around the Montreal Forum ice made the front page of nearly every sports section in Canada. Obviously, they've made up.

The two youngest Hunters got to play seven games together with Washington in 1992–93, but are once again part of the same team. Dale and

Dave Hunter was a member of the Edmonton Oilers when they moved from the WHA to the NHL.

Mark are co-owners of the London Knights junior club and the rink it plays in.

Bergeron said Dale was important for the Nordiques' survival at the time.

"If you remember at the time English players did not want to come to play in Quebec," Bergeron said. "'Quebec? People speak French there!' But Dale, he loved it in Quebec and he told everyone 'this is a beautiful place, friendly people, great restaurants.'

"He would sell Quebec to other English players. He helped make it easier for English players."

When the Nords dealt him to the Washington Capitals, it took years—and a relocation to Denver—for the franchise to recover.

That infamous Hunter tenacity sometimes plunged over the line, going from hard and fair to downright dirty. For a brutal hit from behind on the Islanders' Pierre Turgeon in the spring of 1993, after Turgeon had scored a crucial goal in sending the Caps to the golf course for the summer, Dale received a 21-game suspension to open the next season.

"There are some things you do in the heat of the moment you regret later," said Hunter, who was named captain of the Caps the next year. "That was one of them."

These men from these four families share so many characteristics. "If there is a correlation," reasons Dale Hunter, "it's the influence the parents had on the kids; a sense of work ethic instilled in all of us at an early age.

"The Plagers all played hard. The Sutters all played hard. Dave, Mark, and I played hard. People maybe didn't talk about it as much because of their great talent, but believe me the Stastnys played hard, too."

They are special, these hockey-playing dynasties, blessed with ability and an inner drive that was nurtured in environments conducive to three or more from the same family reaching high enough, pushing hard enough, to play at the same time in the best league in their sport on the planet.

"It comes down to morals and values," contends Brian Sutter with typical bluntness. "It comes down to what you're taught growing up. And we were taught not to cheat ourselves or anyone else.

"We in our family were taught—and all these [brothers] were taught—to care and to try and not to cut corners and to compete like hell all the time. And if at the end of the day, that wasn't enough, you just shook the other guy's hand and you said 'well done.' That's often a hard thing to do."

Especially when the other guy happens to be your brother.

The Hunters were known for their feistiness on the ice. Dale racked up over 3,500 penalty minutes in 1,407 games.

Oh Brother 3

Brothers Joe and Brian Mullen escaped New York's infamous Hell's Kitchen and went on to enjoy fine careers in the NHL. Joe won the Stanley Cups with the Calgary Flames and Pittsburgh Penguins.

O F THE 41 PLAYERS who performed in the NHL during the 1923–4 season, 14—more than 34 percent—had or would have brothers who played major-league hockey.

An outsider might find these figures fascinating, even somewhat astonishing. To anyone familiar with the brotherhood of hockey, they will come as no surprise at all.

"Hockey is the ultimate team game," explained Darryl Sutter.

And since the best teams form a tight, familial bond within their ranks, who better than to supply the adhesive for this bond than family members?

Since the first pucks were dropped more than a century ago, brothers have impacted hockey more than any other sport. In the game's infancy, all-brother teams were commonplace in the amateur leagues, like the Schnarrs of Kitchener, Ontario, whose ranks

Joe Mullen played 17 seasons in the NHL, amassing 1,063 points in 1,062 career games. He won three Stanley Cups and also twice won the Lady Byng Trophy as the player who best combined skill and gentlemanly play.

Brian Mullen moved straight from college hockey to the NHL and scored 24 goals in his rookie season. He went on to tally 622 points in the NHL, but his career was cut short by health problems.

included future Boston Bruin Werner Schnarr, and the Bigelow brothers, who built their own rink on their farm between Treherne and Holland, Manitoba, and invited challenges from all comers.

Among hockey's elite, brothers have won NHL scoring titles. They've started leagues together, lifted the Stanley Cup as teammates, and fought for it as opponents. Siblings have faced each other from opposing benches, even replaced one another there, and beaten each other with pucks and fists.

Brothers have filled every role in the game and come to play it from every corner of the hockey world. But nowhere is brotherly love more apparent in the annals of hockey than in Kirkland Lake, Ontario.

Detroit likes to call itself Hockeytown and even copyrighted the name. Toronto is considered the center of the hockey universe, although Montrealers will doggedly debate this assessment. But when it comes to sibling rivalry, all burgs take a back seat to Kirkland Lake, the undisputed hockey family town.

Founded in 1911 after a gold strike brought prospectors from across the land seeking their claim, it became Canada's largest gold-producing area. It also developed into a veritable gold mine of hockey talent, producing many of the game's household names, several of whom came from the same household.

The town proved a haven for hockey scouts from the 1940s to the 1960s, as NHL bird dogs unearthed their own cache of mineral resources, prompting Leafs' play-by-play announcer Foster Hewitt to label Kirkland Lake, "The town that made the NHL famous."

Ted Lindsay, a Hall of Fame left winger for the Detroit Red Wings, was raised in Kirkland Lake, and followed his father Bert to the NHL, as did Mike Walton, a flashy center who won Cups with Boston and Toronto. His dad Bobby skated with the

(following pages) Both Mickey Redmond and Ken Dryden faced off against their brothers in the NHL.

Jean Potvin joined brother Denis in hoisting the Stanley Cup twice with the New York Islanders.

Canadiens for four games in 1943–44, and Mike's brother Bob played in the World Hockey Association.

Eddie Redmond performed in the minor pro ranks and groomed both of his sons, Dick and Mickey, for NHL careers. Mickey was a two-time 50-goal scorer and captured a pair of Cups.

Dick Duff, a solid left winger for 18 seasons, won multiple championships with Toronto and Montreal, but younger brother Les lived up (or should that be down?) to his name, and stayed in the minors for 15 years.

Larry and Wayne Hillman combined to patrol the blue line for 37 pro seasons and performed as teammates with the Minnesota North Stars, Philadelphia Flyers, and the WHA's Cleveland Crusaders. A third Hillman brother, Floyd, born in the southwestern Ontario hamlet of Ruthven, also skated in the NHL for Boston.

But it was another trio of defensemen from Kirkland Lake who left their mark on hockey. And sometimes, all over each other.

Around town, folks knew Gus Plager as "Squirrel," because of the three nuts he kept at home, Barclay, Bob, and Billy. But the road Barclay paved was one that covered many a hard mile. Barclay established an OHA junior A season-penalty record, sitting out 252 minutes for the Petes in 1958–59.

The Royals visited Peterborough on February 9, 1961. Late in the third period, Bob, the Guelph enforcer, met up with Barclay, Peterborough's policeman, and they decided it was time to lay down the law. The burly defensemen exchanged cross-checks, slashes, fisticuffs, everything except brotherly love.

"We probably had one of the biggest fights ever in junior," is Bob's recollection of that night. "We fought quite a bit on the ice, then we went to the penalty box and we fought. Then we fought in the

Denis Potvin captained the Islanders to four Stanley Cups in the early 1980s and won the Norris Trophy three times as the league's best defenseman.

runway to the dressing rooms after we were thrown out of the game."

"Just a little family tiff," was how the late Barclay once recalled the brotherly brawl. After the game, Barclay walked toward Bob outside the Guelph dressing room, and Bob's teammates backed off, fearing they'd get caught up in the rematch. But this time, all Barclay wanted to exchange was pleasantries and invited Bob out for a bite to eat.

Anyone who has shared a house with a sibling knows that snits happen. If you didn't fight with your brother, it was because you were an only child. And while fighting each other on the ice might seem strange, it's not that uncommon.

Charlie and Lionel Conacher, the first brothers to be named to the first all-star team, also tangled in a game after Lionel took liberties with a Leaf youngster. "Nobody messes with my teammates," Charlie said later. "Not even my brother."

Wayne and Keith Primeau once dropped the gloves in the spirit of the game.

More recently, Keith and Wayne Primeau dropped the mitts with each other during an NHL game, exemplifying that the brotherhood of hockey remains vastly superior to the brotherhood of blood, a religion all hockey siblings preach.

"Family is for the off-season," explained Brent Sutter. "You were brothers off the ice, not on the ice," agreed Bob Plager. "It wasn't strange to fight with (Barclay). If you had to do it, you had to do it."

Phil and Tony Esposito never exchanged a punch on the ice, but they battled every time they faced each other.

Phil Esposito posted staggering numbers during his NHL career, finishing with 717 goals and 1,590 points. Both rank among the highest totals in history.

In the early 1970s, Phil, a center with Boston, was the NHL's most prolific shooter, winning five Art Ross Trophies from 1969 to 1974. Meanwhile, Tony emerged as the game's pre-eminent stopper, capturing three Vezina Trophies.

Tony's big break came during the 1968–69 season after injuries idled Habs' regulars Gump Worsley and Rogie Vachon. But his first start was against Phil and the Bruins, the first time the brothers would oppose each other in a game.

Tony Esposito began his Hall of Fame career with the Montreal Canadiens but made his mark with the Chicago Blackhawks, registering 423 wins.

"He played junior and I played college," Tony said. "Before that, we were always on the same team."

The affair ended in a 2-2 tie, with Phil scoring two. The next year, Tony won the Calder and Vezina Trophies, but Phil scored a hat trick in the playoff series opener en route to a first-round Boston sweep.

"When it comes to goaltenders, I wouldn't even give my own brother a break," said Phil, who would nonetheless leap to Tony's defense when he heard any disparaging remarks by teammates about his ability.

Many an NHL netminding career was launched through the worst intentions of an older brother. Pat Jablonski, who toiled for five NHL teams in eight seasons during the 1990s, was two when he was first pushed between the pipes by his brother Bobby, seven years his senior, because Bobby and his buddies required a moving target for their shooting gallery.

Howard Lockhart never was joined by his brother in the NHL ranks, but the lament of, "Oh, brother," certainly played a frustrating role in his netminding career. On January 14, 1922, while tending goal for the Hamilton Tigers in a 10-6 loss to Montreal, Sprague and Odie Cleghorn of the Canadiens each scored four, producing an NHL record for goals in one game by brothers.

Corb Denneny of the Toronto St. Patricks beat Lockhart six times in a 10-3 victory January 26, 1921. Less than two months later, Corb's brother Cy put six pucks past Lockhart, leading his Senators to a 12-5 triumph. Both of the Dennenys netted Stanley Cup–winning goals—Corb for the Toronto Arenas in 1917–18 and Cy for the Senators in 1926–7, joining the Richards as the only brothers to cement Cup victories for their teams. Maurice

In 1944-45, Maurice "the Rocket" Richard became the first player to score 50 goals in a season, accomplishing the feat in 50 games.

Richard bagged Montreal's Cup-clinching tally in 1955–56, while younger brother Henri turned the trick twice for the Habs in 1965–66 and 1970–71. Between them, Maurice (eight) and Henri (eleven) own more Stanley Cup rings than any siblings, winning five in a row from 1956 to 1960 as teammates.

About 15 years earlier, the NHL's first all-brother line took to the ice in Chicago, where Max and Doug Bentley were joined in the Blackhawks' lineup by younger brother Reggie for 11 games during the 1942–43 season.

Henri Richard, "the Pocket Rocket," spent his entire 20-year career with Montreal, accumulating 1,046 points in 1,259 games.

(following pages) A native of Montreal, Maurice Richard joined the Canadiens in 1942. He went on to win eight Stanley Cups and in doing so became the greatest player in the franchise's history.

While brother Maurice was known for his fiery temper, Henri Richard was a more gentlemanly player. In 1974 he won the Bill Masterton Trophy, awarded to the player who best exemplifies perseverance, sportsmanship, and dedication to hockey.

On February 22, 1981, the Stastnys led the Nords to an 11-7 rout of the Capitals at Washington. Peter tallied four goals and four assists, while Anton knocked three pucks into the net and contributed five helpers, to give each sibling the NHL standard for points in a road game.

"To set an NHL record was very special, but to share it with your brother, that's a pretty big thing," Peter said. "The amazing thing about it was we'd played in Vancouver two nights earlier and both of us had three goals and three assists (in a 9-3 Quebec win). We combined for 28 points in two games and were named co-players of the week."

The previous mark of seven points in a road game was established December 5, 1924, by the Hamilton Tigers' Red Green against Toronto. He and his adopted brother Wilfred (Shorty) Green were teammates from 1923–24 through 1926–27 with the Tigers and New York Americans.

In 1924–25, Red led the NHL with 15 assists. Shorty, whose career was ended when he lost a kidney after absorbing a devastating check from Rangers defenseman Taffy Abel in a 1927 game, is still famous in Hamilton. The diminutive, green drinking fountains that populate the city are called "Shorty Greens," a fact that could be seen as an amazing tribute, considering it was the Green brothers who played a key role in the demise of NHL hockey in Hamilton.

After leading the Tigers to a first-place finish in 1924–25, the Greens led a strike over unpaid bonus money. The club was suspended and sold during the off-season to New York interests, where the Tigers became the New York Americans.

Red, on the left wing, and Shorty, on the right side, formed two-thirds of the NHL's best forward line featuring siblings until New York's second NHL squad, the Rangers, came into existence in 1926–27.

Pete and Frank Mahovlich played together for both the
Red Wings and Canadiens. They won two Stanley Cups as
teammates in Montreal.

Family values were important to the Mahovlich brothers, Frank and Pete.

Ken Dryden burst on to the scene as a rookie during the 1970-71 playoffs. He led his team to the Stanley Cup while winning the Conn Smythe Trophy as MVP of the playoffs.

Coach Lester Patrick put together his A Line, named after New York's A-train subway line, with center Frank Boucher working between Bill and Bun Cook. The NHL's longest-running forward combination, skating as a unit for ten seasons, would all make the Hall.

Brother acts were quite familiar to Boucher, who was one of four siblings to skate in the NHL. Frank, who won two Cups, captured the Lady Byng as the league's most sportsmanlike player seven times between 1927–28 and 1934–35, so the NHL decided to give him the trophy and have a new one minted.

Dave Dryden did not have as successful a career as brother Ken, but the two have the distinction of being the only brothers to oppose each other as goalies in an NHL game.

George (Buck) Boucher, a winner of four Cups, was a rugged, skillful defenseman who also earned Hall status and was the opposite of Frank in on-ice behavior. He led the NHL in penalty minutes in 1924–25 and retired in 1932 as its career penalty-minute leader.

Billy Boucher, a left winger with three NHL clubs over seven seasons, followed George with 92 minutes in 1924–25. George had 95.

Paul and Steve Kariya were both standouts at the University of Maine. Paul was drafted fourth overall by the Anaheim Mighty Ducks, and Steve signed as a free agent with the Vancouver Canucks.

While brother Paul is a perennial all-star, Steve Kariya has appeared in just 65 games over three NHL seasons.

Bobby, a center with the Habs that same season, was a pacifist like Frank, never visiting the penalty box in 11 NHL games with Montreal. All four Bouchers also share another common bond—inscription on the Cup. Billy and Bobby joined their brothers when the Habs won it all in 1923–24.

En route to the title, they downed Frank's Vancouver Maroons of the Pacific Coast League in the 1923–24 Cup semifinals. In the deciding game of that best-of-three set, the Habs took a 2-1 verdict, a pair of goals from Billy overcoming a solo marker from Frank.

"I was walking down the street after that game and there was a placard outside a shop which read, 'Final score: Billy Boucher 2, Frank Boucher 1,'" Frank recalled years later.

Three sets of brothers appeared on the ice in an NHL game on Dec. 1, 1940. Chicago, featuring Bob and Bill Carse, downed Lynn and Murray (Muzz) Patrick and Neil and Mac Colville of the Rangers 4-1.

But the Sutters are the NHL brothers scoring champs, combining for 1,320 goals, ahead of Bobby and Dennis Hull (913), the Richards (902), Wayne and Brent Gretzky (895), Frank and Peter Mahovlich (821), and Gordie and Vic Howe (804).

Among that group, Brent Sutter (363 goals) is the only younger sibling to be the top family sniper. The gap between older and younger brother is especially evident with the Gretzkys, where Wayne scored 894 times and the Howes, who got 801 of their goals from Gordie.

Sometimes, though, the younger sibling sets the pace. Andy Bathgate earned Hall status, scoring 349 times, while older brother Frank played just two NHL games, never denting the twine.

Roman Hamrlik broke into the NHL at 18 with the Tampa Bay Lightning in 1992–93, the same season his older brother Martin was toiling in the

After winning the Hobey Baker Award as the top player in American College Hockey, Paul Kariya has become one of the most dangerous players in the NHL.

Tomas Kaberle was an eighth-round draft pick on the Maple Leafs in 1996. He has become a mainstay on their blue line.

junior ranks with the Ontario Hockey's League's Oshawa Generals. Tomas Kaberle earned a spot on the Leafs' defense in 1998–99, one season before his brother Frantisek, five years his senior, made the NHL grade in Los Angeles and later, Atlanta.

Ron and Rich Sutter were the first twins to suit up for a game in 1983–84 with Philadelphia. Six

Both Maurice Richard and Gordie Howe are among the best players the game has seen. Howe's sons Mark and Marty followed him to the NHL; Richard's brother Henri did the same.

Frantisek Kaberle broke into the league with the Los Angeles Kings in 1999, a year after his brother Tomas surfaced with the Maple Leafs.

Twins Peter and Chris Ferraro have scored at every level of hockey, but both have been unable to make their mark in the NHL.

years later, they were joined by New Jersey Devil forwards Peter and Patrik Sundstrom, who playfully switched sweaters during a game against the Rangers that season. Chris and Peter Ferraro followed suit with the Rangers, Pittsburgh Penguins, and Washington Capitals, and Daniel and Henrik Sedin now skate with the Vancouver Canucks.

Another pair of twins—Joel and Henrik Lundqvist—played for Sweden in the 2001 world junior championship. Both were 2000 NHL draft picks. Henrik, a netminder, went to the Rangers, while Dallas tabbed Joel, a center.

No twins have joined each other on a Cup winner, but 27 Cup champions have included brother combinations, beginning with the first NHL title holders, the 1917–18 Toronto Arenas, who were coached by Dick Carroll and trained by his brother Frank. The Cleghorns and Bouchers, with the 1923–24 Canadiens, were the NHL's first champion brother acts.

Brian is the second Sutter to coach Chicago after Darryl, but no brothers shared the coaching fate that the Murrays experienced with Washington.

Bryan took over as coach of the Caps in 1981 and led the club to its first playoff appearance and a record 107-point season in 1985–86. Bryan hired younger brother Terry to be his assistant in 1982, marking the first time brothers had coached an NHL team together.

Vancouver Canucks' general manager Brian Burke pulled a draft-day deal in 1999, allowing him to pick twins Henrik and Daniel Sedin simultaneously with the second and third picks overall.

Together since day one, Daniel and Henrik Sedin were
superstars in Sweden during their junior days, making
them highly regarded prospects.

Terry Murray was an assistant coach to older brother
Bryan with the Washington Capitals. When Bryan was fired,
Terry stepped in and took over the head coaching duties.

Bryan Murray has coached the Capitals, Red Wings, Florida Panthers, and the Anaheim Mighty Ducks.

"It was because he was a good coach, not because he was my brother," said Bryan, who was also Terry's teacher at Pontiac Secondary School in Shawville, Quebec, where he coached Terry on the football, volleyball, and hockey teams. "I always thought he'd be a real good coaching prospect."

Bryan probably didn't think that Terry's first NHL head coaching job would come at his own expense, but that's what happened January 15, 1990, when Washington GM David Poile fired Bryan and replaced him with Terry. "I was uncomfortable with the idea of replacing Bryan," Terry said, "but David told me, 'look, the change has been made. Somebody is going to take the job.' I talked it over with Bryan and he encouraged me to do it.

"As a coach, it's inevitable that you will be replaced one day. We both looked at it as part of the game."

In 1995–96, Bryan led the Florida Panthers to the Cup final as general manager, and Terry coached the Philadelphia Flyers there the following spring. Bryan hired Terry to be Florida's coach in 1998, and they worked in unison for two more seasons, until they were fired together on December 28, 2000.

"I think our time together, both in Washington and Florida, only strengthened our relationship as brothers," Terry said. "Dealing with the ups and downs that coaching involves, being there for each other, it really helped to develop a strong bond."

Each continues to work within the NHL ranks —Bryan as general manager and coach of the Anaheim Mighty Ducks and Terry as a pro scout with the Flyers.

"We talk all the time," Bryan said. "We've always had a very open relationship. If he sees something, Terry's not afraid to point out suggestions in regards to players on my team. If I pick up something while watching his team, I'll tell him about it."

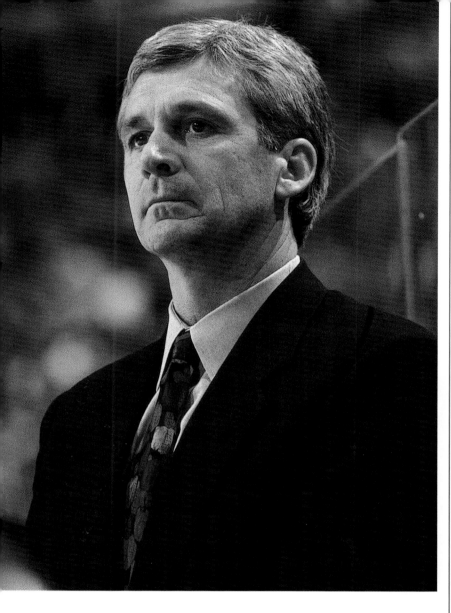

Terry Murray followed in the footsteps of brother Bryan coaching Washington, Florida, and the Philadelphia Flyers.

Matt Pavelich never was asked to take his brother's position. Their working relationship required that he keep his brother in line. Pavelich skated 23 seasons as an NHL official, becoming the first linesman to earn Hall recognition, pulling on a striped shirt at the same time that his brother Marty was playing with the Red Wings.

There were no league restrictions preventing Matt from working any of Marty's games, meaning that sometimes, he'd have to get between his brother and an opponent to prevent an altercation.

"In those instances, I'd always grab the other guy and let the other linesman take Marty," Matt said.

Marcel Dionne was one of the most prolific scorers in NHL history. He was inducted into the Hall of Fame in 1992 and appeared in 1,100 more games than brother Gilbert.

Art Skov was an NHL referee and linesman when his brother Glen was playing for Detroit and Chicago. Dan McCourt still works the lines in the NHL, years after his brother Dale stopped playing in the league.

The Costellos were another brother combination who traveled a unique path. After a brief NHL fling in the mid-1950s, Murray Costello put his hockey brain to use as president of the Canadian Amateur Hockey Association. Meanwhile, brother Les, a Cup winner with Toronto in 1947–48, became a Father—giving up the NHL in 1950 to enter the priesthood.

Gilbert Dionne is 19 years younger than his legendary brother Marcel. He entered the league with the Canadiens the year after Marcel retired.

Les helped found the Flying Fathers, a group of hockey-playing priests who mixed entertaining hockey and comedy to became a sort of white-collared version of the Harlem Globetrotters, raising millions of dollars for charitable causes, performing under the slogan, 'Playing and praying for a better world.'

The pugnacious McSorleys gave headaches to others and hold the unofficial sibling standard for stupefying suspensions. Playing for Toledo of the IHL in 1985, Chris McSorley was suspended for the remainder of the season for biting off the tip of the nose of Indianapolis's Marc Magnan during a fight. While playing for the Bruins in 1999–2000, older brother Marty was sentenced to a year on the sidelines after clubbing Vancouver's Donald Brashear.

That same season, New Jersey Devils' Scott Niedermayer was assessed a ten-game sitdown after taking his hickory to the head of Panthers' forward Peter Worrell. That put Scott's younger brother Rob, a Panthers' center, in the uncomfortable position of having to choose sides between brother and teammate.

Scott Niedermayer, a defenseman, was the third overall pick with the New Jersey Devils in 1991.

Rob, the younger of the Niedermayer brothers, was taken fifth overall two years after his brother broke into the league with the Devils.

The eldest of the three hockey-playing Broten brothers, Neal played 1,099 NHL games and was a member of the 1980 Miracle on Ice team.

When Paul and Neal Broten skated with the Dallas Stars in 1993–94, they were the first brother act to perform in the franchise's lineup since Neal and Aaron Broten played for the then Minnesota North Stars in 1989–90.

Bob Sabourin played one game for the Leafs in 1952, the same club his younger brother Gary would play for in 1974–75. Ric Seiling made his NHL debut with the Sabres in 1977–78, which was the second-last of 17 NHL campaigns for his older brother Rod.

Paul Broten, a right winger, played 322 games between 1989 and 1996 with the Rangers, Blues, and Dallas Stars.

132

At Detroit's 2000–01 training camp, rookie hopeful Tim Verbeek, 20, battled for a job alongside older brother Pat, 36, an 18-year NHL veteran. Mark Greig broke into the NHL with the Hartford Whalers in 1990–91, 16 seasons after his older brother Bruce played his final NHL season for the California Golden Seals.

Tim Sheehy won a silver medal with the United States at the 1972 Winter Olympics. Twenty years later, younger brother Neil was on the U.S. defense at the world championships.

Brotherly love has often been combined with love for country on the international hockey stage. The Holiks—Jiri and Jaroslav, the latter father of current NHLer Bobby Holik—won five Olympic medals for Czechoslovakia.

When Canada put its hockey reputation on the line in the 1972 Summit Series against the Soviet Union, brothers played key roles in Canada's eventual 4-3-1 verdict in the eight-game set. Phil Esposito led all scorers with 13 points, while Tony posted two wins and a tie in four starts. After a stunning 7-3 loss in the opener of the series, Canada was clinging to a 2-1 advantage in Game 2 when Peter and Frank Mahovlich each tallied third-period markers.

Back in North America, the Timmins, Ontario, brothers would win a combined ten Cups with the Leafs and Canadiens, and were Montreal teammates for title years in 1971 and 1973. The "Big M" Frank and "Little M" Peter (who was actually five inches taller) played a total of 2,290 regular-season and playoff games with 2,066 points.

The Reichels both participated in the 2002 Winter Olympics in Salt Lake City, but at opposite ends of the rink. Robert suited up for the Czech Republic, while his younger brother Martin performed for Germany.

Aaron Broten entered the league with the Colorado Rockies during the 1980-81 season. He went on to play 748 games with six teams.

During his pro hockey career, Robert Reichel has moved back and forth between Europe and the NHL. He managed a personal best 40 goals and 93 points with Calgary in 1993-94.

"He's been living in Germany for 13 to 14 years and is using a German passport," Robert explained. "I also played against him at the World Championships in 1996 and 1997."

The Reichels followed in the paths of Frantisek Tikal, who played for Czechoslovakia in the 1960 Winter Games in Squaw Valley, California, against his brother Zdenek, a member of the Australian team.

The Hanson brothers also attempted to cross international boundaries to perform for the United States at the 1928 Olympiad in St. Moritz, Switzerland, but got caught in a technicality, as they weren't Americans.

The team from Minnesota's Augsburg College was put forth to represent the United States in the Olympics, a squad that included five Hanson siblings—Julius, Joe, Louis, Emil, and Oscar, the latter two future NHLers.

Unfortunately, they were also all residents of Camrose, Alberta, and held Canadian citizenship. When this was discovered by the chairman of the U.S. Olympic Committee—a certain Major General Douglas MacArthur, who later gained fame for returning to the Philippines during World War II— they were rejected. The United States did not ice a team that year.

A half century later, America would produce its own set of Hanson Brothers and they, too, would gain international notoriety. In 1977, Universal Studios released a slapstick comedy about a minor-league hockey team. *Slap Shot* starred Oscar-winner Paul Newman. But it was the Hanson brothers who stole the show, with their horn-rimmed glasses, foil-wrapped fists, and the general mayhem they created between the boards.

Two of these celluloid legends were actual brothers—Steve and Jeff Carlson from Virginia, Minnesota—and the third was an actual Hanson— Dave Hanson of Cumberland, Wisconsin. And all three were professional hockey players long before they became actors.

Dave Hanson performed in the NHL with Detroit and Minnesota, while Steve Carlson was a Los Angeles King. Jeff Carlson played for the Minnesota Fighting Saints in the WHA.

Brothers Steve and Jeff Carlson, along with Dave Hanson, brought hockey to the American public as the Hanson brothers in the movie *Slap Shot.* All three played pro hockey, Dave Hanson and Jeff Carlson in the NHL, and Steve Carlson in the WHA.

"Most of what we put in the film was taken from the real-life experiences of Dave Hanson and my brothers Jeff and Jack when they played for the [North American Hockey League's] Johnstown Jets," Steve Carlson explained.

Jack Carlson also performed in the NHL with St. Louis and the North Stars, but a recall to the big leagues cost him his shot at Hollywood legend status.

Hockey Night in Canada broadcaster and former NHL coach Harry Neale tutored all three Carlsons and Hanson in the WHA and admits the movie is a case of art imitating life.

"When I was coaching the Minnesota Fighting Saints, we scheduled open tryout camps across the state, more for publicity purposes than any thought that we'd find players," Neale recalled. "The three Carlsons showed up at one camp, just like the first scene in the movie, wearing their hockey jackets, with the goofy smiles and the thick glasses. I looked at [GM] Glen Sonmor and said, 'Who the hell are these guys?'"

"Well, when they got out on the ice, they just beat the bejesus out of everybody. And they kept doing it, through rookie camp, through main training camp, until they'd earned contracts."

A sequel, *Slap Shot 2: Breaking the Ice,* was released direct to video on March 26, 2002. The Carlson brothers were never better than average pro players, but the fictional siblings they portrayed on screen granted them cult status. This did nothing, however, to enhance their notoriety as hockey goons, which had been determined years before.

"We had a reputation long before the movie came out," Jeff Carlson said.

Mark and Marty, sons of the legendary Gordie Howe, had the unique experience of playing pro hockey alongside their Hall of Fame father.

Boris Mironov was a second-round pick of the Winnipeg Jets in 1992. He was traded to the Edmonton Oilers midway through his rookie campaign. After six seasons with the Oilers, he was traded to the Chicago Blackhawks.

Dmitri, the elder of the Moscow-born Mironov brothers, hoisted the Stanley Cup in 1998 as a member of the Detroit Red Wings.

Brothers Paiement

Rosaire Paiement joined the NHL with the expansion Philadelphia Flyers in 1967. His NHL numbers were modest (100 points in 190 games), but he went on to have a successful career in the WHA.

Wilf Paiement is one of the few players, other than Wayne Gretzky, to wear number 99 in the NHL. The brother of Rosaire should also be remembered for his play, as he tallied 814 points during his career.

Fathers and Sons

4

During the strike-shortened 1994–95 season, Marty McSorley, Wayne Gretzky, Paul Coffey, and Mark Messier went to Europe as members of the Ninety-Niners; they brought their dads along for the ride.

F OR MUCH of its history, hockey's key relationship has been the one between father and son.

The bonding would start early. With the first tentative step on the local pond or on a painstakingly flooded backyard rink. At the breakfast table, with discussions of the previous night's NHL scores. In

front of the television or, in a lost era, crowded around the wireless.

A family pleasure, to be sure, but one shared most acutely by males because until the recent age of enlightenment, hockey was a game played by men.

So, it's not surprising that a father with an extraordinary aptitude for hockey would pass it on to a son, through heredity, a stimulating environment, or a hybrid of both. When a family climate fosters an interest in the game and provides a hockey-friendly gene pool, there would seem to be a better chance for the offspring to succeed in hockey.

Although three families— the Howes, Hulls, and Patricks —tend to dominate the landscape, there have been at least 69 different fathers who have played in the NHL and then had a son follow them to the world's best hockey league.

Those father-son pairings had a diverse range of success, exemplified by two tandems whose fathers played for the Chicago Blackhawks and whose sons spent part of their careers with the Detroit Red Wings.

The Hulls, father Bobby and son Brett, each scored more than 600 NHL goals, Bobby for all but six with the Chicago Blackhawks and Brett for four teams, including the Wings. Lou Holmes and his

Gordie, Mark, and Marty Howe made hockey history in 1980 when they joined forces as members of the Hartford Whalers. The Howes remain the only father-son combo to play together in the NHL.

Pat Stapleton, a four-time NHL all-star, enjoyed a ten-year NHL career with the Bruins and Blackhawks. He teamed with defense partner Bill White to help Canada defeat Russia in the 1972 Summit Series.

son Chuck each scored one NHL goal in their careers. Lou played a total of 59 games for Chicago from 1931 to 1933 and Chuck played 23 for Detroit in 1958–59 and 1960–61.

Career numbers, though, can never paint an accurate picture. Consider, for instance, the modest NHL accomplishments of the Palazzaris of Eveleth, Minnesota, the shinny hotbed and home of the U.S. Hockey Hall of Fame.

Mike, son of former Blackhawk defenseman Pat Stapleton, has appeared in 697 NHL games with eight different teams, including Chicago.

On his way to the Hall of Fame, Bryan Hextall guided the New York Rangers to the Stanley Cup in 1940 and twice led the NHL in goals.

Aldo played only 35 NHL games, all in 1943–44, and his son played only 108 from 1974 to 1979. Both men were short of stature—Aldo five foot seven, Doug only five foot five—but long on heart.

With his career off to a promising start, Aldo was forced to retire after that one season because he lost an eye during an exhibition game. His son was also very seriously injured, during a practice with the minor league Kansas City Blues. A teammate's skate severed his lip, knocked out 11 teeth, and broke his jaw in six places.

He should have retired but stayed on to twice lead the Central Hockey League in goals, assists, and points and was recently chosen as the most out-standing player in CHL history. In 1999, he was appointed executive director of USA Hockey and is probably bound for the U.S. Hall of Fame in his hometown.

Given the circumstantial, and probable genetic, head start that sons of players enjoy, it's a little startling that with more than 5,200 men having played at least one NHL game up to 2002, only 69 have fathered sons who also reached the top level of their dad's profession.

That tiny fraction may be explained several ways: only a filament-thin percentage of all kids who play hockey ever play pro at any level, let alone the NHL; a large number of the 5,200 NHLers played in the last 25 years, so more talented offspring may be on their way into the elite ranks; and perhaps many hockey sons, like children of other professionals, chose their own career path and not their father's.

Of those 69 fathers, two also have had grandsons get that far.

Hall-of-Famer Bryan Hextall led the New York Rangers to the 1940 Stanley Cup and was the NHL's goal-scoring leader that season and in 1940–41. His sons Bryan Jr. and Dennis each played more than

500 games during the 1960s and 1970s and were teammates on the Minnesota North Stars in the 1975–76 season, Bryan Jr.'s last in the NHL.

And early NHLer Lester Patrick, a hockey man of mythical proportions, was GM of the 1940 Cup-winning Rangers when his two sons, Lynn and Muzz, were stars of the team. Lester is also one of eight former NHLers who had more than one son follow him into the league as a player. Two of those eight men had three sons reach the NHL.

Goalie Harvey Bennett was just 19 when he was called up to play 25 games for the 1944–45 Bruins.

Walter Gretzky was an integral part of son Wayne's development both as a hockey player and as a person. The stories of Walter's backyard rinks in Brantford, Ontario, have become hockey lore.

He was sent back to the minors and never played in the NHL again, but three of his sons did. Curt had a solid NHL career, with 152 goals in 580 games, including two 30-goal seasons; Harvey Jr. played 268 games and was Curt's teammate on three teams in 1978–79, the St. Louis Blues and Team USA twice.

Along with brother Bryan, Dennis Hextall followed his father's lead and made his way to the NHL. He played parts of 13 seasons with six organizations.

Ron Hextall, son of Bryan Jr., exploded on the NHL scene in 1987. The volatile netminder won both the Vezina and Conn Smythe Trophies in his rookie year.

(previous pages) Bill Dineen had three boys who made it to the NHL – Kevin, Gord, and Peter. Bill played five years with the Detroit Red Wings, scoring 51 goals.

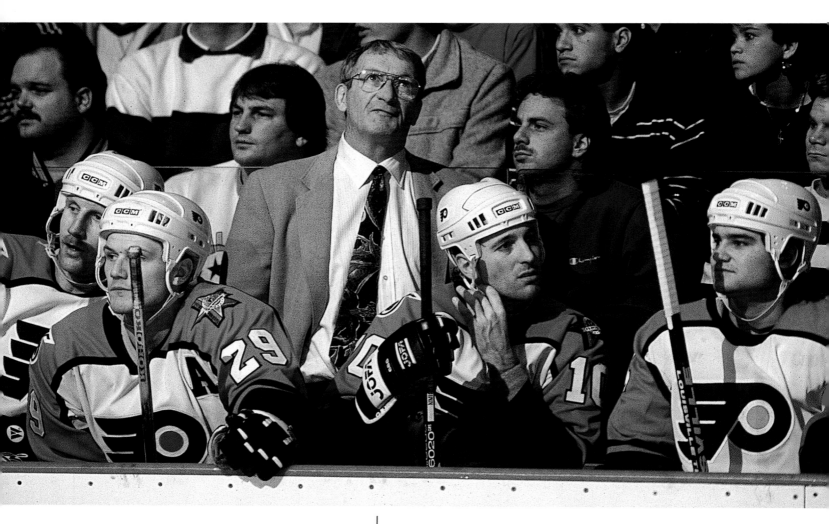

Bill Dineen coached son Kevin with the Philadelphia Flyers.

Their brother Bill played seven games for the Bruins that season, and 24 more for New England the following year, before his career ended in the minors.

Bill Dineen, who became a well-respected coach, won two Cups in five NHL years, mostly with Detroit in the mid-1950s. His sons Kevin, Gord, and Peter broke into the league in the 1980s, although Peter played only 13 games. The Dineen brothers never played on the same NHL team, but Kevin did spend two seasons as a Flyer when his dad coached in Philadelphia from 1991 to 1993.

155

Two decades earlier, Dineen was just beginning his coaching career when his lineup suddenly included the most famous father-son combination in hockey history.

Kevin Dineen learned much from his father Bill, a former player and coach. He played 1,184 games, the majority with the Flyers and Whalers.

A stay-at-home defenseman, Gord Dineen played parts of 13 seasons in the NHL scoring just 16 goals.

Dineen's old Detroit buddy Gordie Howe would eventually become the only man to play on an NHL team with his sons (Hartford, 1979–80), but Gordie, Mark, and Marty first suited up together six years earlier for Houston in the WHA.

The 45-year-old Howe came out of a two-year retirement to play for Houston with his sons Marty, 19, and Mark, 18, who had been playing junior hockey in Toronto. Under rules at the time, both were too young for the NHL draft.

Mark Howe was one of the most versatile players the game has seen. He was dangerous, patrolling the wing much like his father Gordie, but his ability to control the pace of the game ultimately made him more valuable as a defenseman.

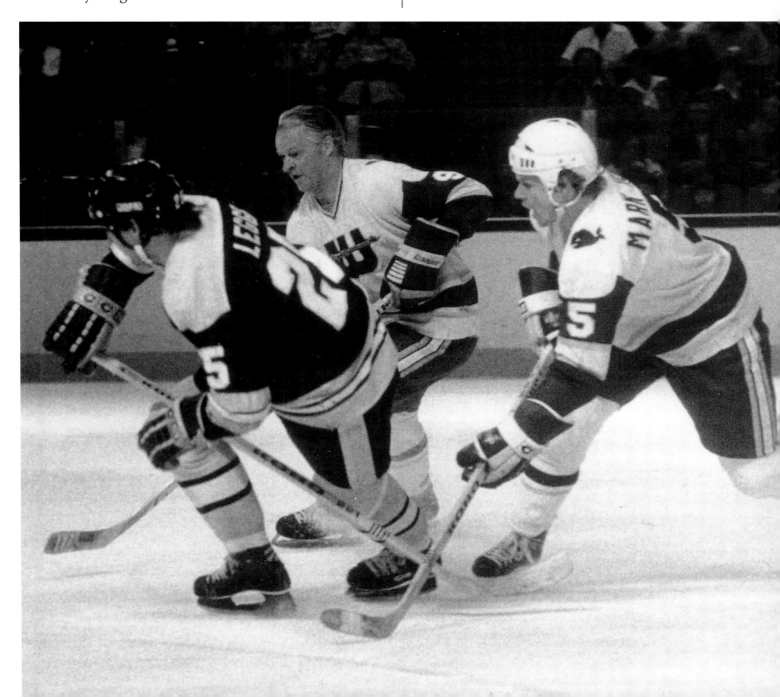

Marty Howe played alongside brother Mark and father Gordie during his days in the WHA. They were reunited in the NHL for six games during the 1979-80 season.

"Colleen [Gordie's wife] gave the WHA the idea to draft the under-aged kids, and that bought me about three or four years more of hockey," recalls Gordie, who's considered by many to be the greatest player in the history of the NHL. "The fun had gone out of the game for me, so I'd retired. I'd had wrist surgery; the team in Detroit couldn't win.

"Colleen was putting the contract together for the kids with Bill Dineen and Doug Harvey, when at the last minute they said, 'what about a third Howe?' They all looked at one another, and suddenly I was about to play again.

"It was halfway comical at first. I was dying. The speed was more than I expected, and I couldn't make or take passes. I told Colleen that this might have been a mistake. But then we started two-a-day practices and I started to feel good."

A psychic told Colleen before that first season in Houston that Gordie would play well, and that she saw two trophies and maybe a championship. The Aeros were WHA champions in 1973–74 (Howe's first year), Gordie was MVP, and Mark rookie of the year.

Although Marty was the least well-regarded of the trio, when the Howes held a family race that season—from one end of the rink to the other and back—it was Marty who won.

In their third season in Houston, Dineen removed Mark from Gordie's line because he wanted his talent and vision back on the blue line, a decision that gave the youngest Howe the versatility to become one of the best all-round players of his era.

After the fourth year, the father and sons became free agents, and it appeared that the family would return to the NHL with Boston. But new Bruins' ownership abruptly tried to reduce their negotiated four-year deal to one, so Colleen, who'd insisted on no bidding war, called the New England

The 1973-74 WHA season saw Gordie Howe take home the MVP award, while son Mark was rookie of the year.

Whalers, and the family stayed in the WHA until New England joined the NHL in 1979, and became the Hartford Whalers.

The only time the Howes started a game as a complete forward line—with Gordie moving to center from right wing—was in 1980 when the Whalers played the Wings in their second-ever NHL visit to Detroit.

"Marty had a temperature of 103 degrees, but there was no way he was going to miss that," Gordie recalled. "That was where we live, where I played, and where the boys grew up."

As kids, Marty and Mark spent hours around their father's workplace, and were welcomed by the other Wings. Sometimes, they would take their complementary tickets and scalp them because they were so well-known at the Olympia that they could just walk past ushers.

Being the son of former goalie Rogie Vachon did not seem to help Nick make it at the NHL level. He appeared in only one game and his name did not find its way onto the score sheet.

"Little buggers," Gordie laughs, confirming the story. "I think the big advantage to them was just growing up around it and seeing the people and how they played. It really helped them. When they were 14 or 15 they used to help sweep the stands at the Olympia and afterwards they'd have six or eight hours of ice all to themselves.

"I think the boys said it best back then: 'Sometimes it's a detriment being Gordie Howe's son, but most of the time it's reeeeallly great.'"

Howe came out of retirement in 1997–98 for a one-game cameo with the International Hockey League Detroit Vipers, to give himself one-game in six different decades!

Many hockey-playing sons of NHLers have a similar, if more muted, feeling. There is usually some kind of balancing act involving the natural skills and invaluable experience taken from the father and the negative aspects of fame in the family. There can be drawbacks in sharing your father with the public, and in facing the implied pressure that accompanies the family name.

Nobody has cleared the latter hurdle with more to spare than Brett Hull. His father Bobby, the Golden Jet, cast a huge, colorful shadow over all of hockey for more than 20 years.

No one has ever played the game with more elan, and he was one of the first superstars of the game's TV era, instantly recognizable by his rippling muscles and radiant smile.

Brett and Bobby share the blond mane, a thunderingly lethal shot, a penchant for outspokenness, and little else, other than an innate ability to score.

Brett's game depends upon escaping detection until he gets open for a pass and a one-timer. Bobby was the guy who made you look at him, whose speed and powerful burst down the left wing attracted

Rogie Vachon won 355 games during his 16-year NHL career and helped to solidify the unstable Los Angeles Kings franchise during the 1970s. Upon retirement, he returned to L.A. where he served as coach, general manager, and chief operating officer of the Kings.

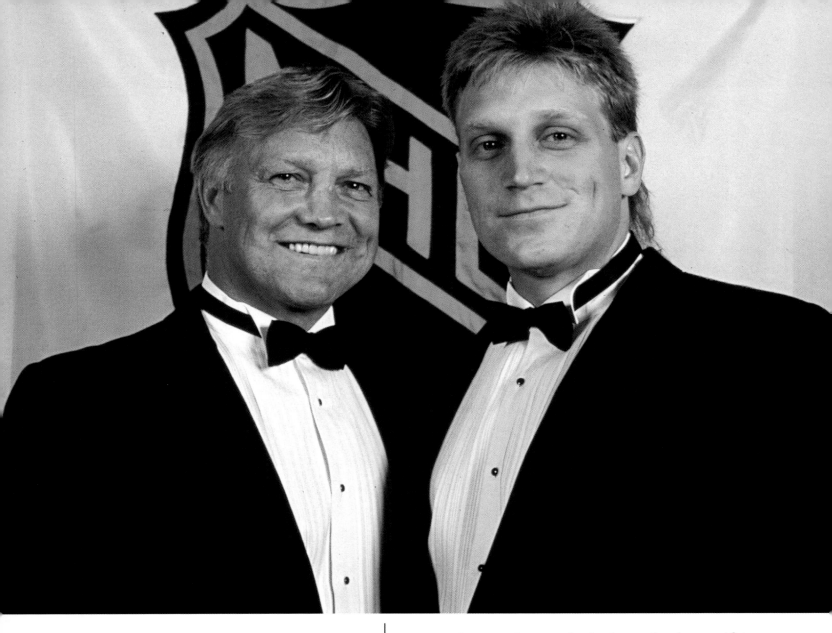

While Bobby Hull is considered to be one of the greatest goal-scorers in the history of the game, his son Brett just may be better. During the the 1999-2000 season Brett scored his 600th goal, making the pair the only father-son combination to reach that amazing plateau.

everyone's attention, and who brought the terrifying slap shot into the game.

"The first time I saw that thing," said Blackhawks goalie Glenn Hall, "I said a prayer of thanks that I didn't have to worry about it."

That shot once paralyzed Hall of Famer Jacques Plante's arm for five minutes.

Bobby graduated from major junior hockey to the NHL at 18, and four years later led Chicago to the 1961 Cup, its last to date. The next season he became the third player ever to score 50 goals, a feat he repeated four times, unheard of in that era.

He was lured to the Winnipeg Jets of the WHA with a $2.75 million contract in 1972, giving the new league instant star power. It was there that Brett became aware of his father's skill and stardom.

"I saw him play a lot, mainly in the WHA," the son recalls. "He was never a guy who told you how to play the game, you watched him. But he was always there to help.

"It was more an emulation thing, mostly what he did for speed. I'm a stealth guy, I wasn't the greatest skater when I was a kid, but I enjoyed shooting."

So much so that when his dad brought him an autographed Guy Lafleur stick from the 1976 Canada Cup, Brett took it out onto the driveway to play ball hockey and shattered it within two hours.

"When I'd give him the dickens about how he played, all of the sudden he'd take the puck and go the length of the ice and put it in," Bobby recalled. "Then he'd skate around to where I was and give me that great [smirk] of his just to say, 'I can do this any time I want.'"

Bobby and Joanne Hull separated when Brett was 15, and he moved to Vancouver with his mother, sister, and brothers. He played some Tier Two in Penticton, B.C., but skipped major junior for a scholarship at the University of Minnesota-Duluth. After two seasons, he joined the Calgary Flames as a low draft choice (117th overall), but his game never found acceptance there.

Despite scoring 26 goals in just 52 games of what was essentially his first full season, Brett was shipped to the Blues in 1988. Over the next six seasons, Hull scored a stunning 380 goals, including 86 in 1990–91, the third-highest total of all time.

He scored against Buffalo's Dominik Hasek in the third overtime of the sixth game of the 1999 finals to give Dallas its first Cup. And at 7:33 of the

In 1990-91, Brett Hull scored a remarkable 86 goals for the St. Louis Blues and has reached the 70 mark three times. He is arguably the best goal-scorer of his generation—a distinction he shares with his father Bobby.

Harold Ballard became one of three owners of the Toronto Maple Leafs in 1961. He was more concerned with the bottom line than the success of the team and the storied Leafs became one of the worst teams in the league while under his control.

third period of a game in Toronto on October 9, 2000, he beat Curtis Joseph for his 611th NHL goal. That was one more than his famous sire, although Bobby did have 303 goals in the WHA.

"He's a better player than his father ever thought of being," a proud Bobby said.

"In our games, there is not a lot in common," Brett added. "I mean, if you remember the way he

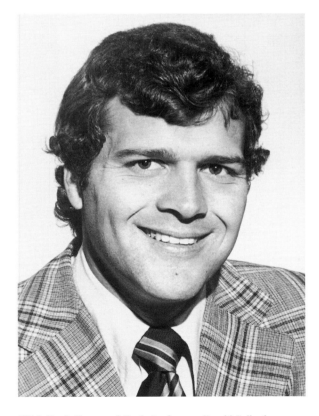

Bill Ballard, the son of Maple Leaf owner Harold Ballard, was the vice-president during the tumultuous years his father owned the club.

164

played, he was strong. I just lumbered around the ice and weaved my way in and out of holes.

"I'm not flashy at all. I look like a plumber and that makes people forget about you. I'm not a big celebrator, either. Those are two good ways of staying out of people's memory banks.

"We were different that way, but in the same sense, I think the personality that I got from him

Norm Dube, a seventh round draft pick of the L.A. Kings, had a cup of coffee with the Kansas City Scouts in the mid 1970s, scoring eight goals.

Christian Dube, like his father Norm, had only a brief stint in the NHL. Despite being a highly touted junior prospect, he managed just one goal in 33 games with the Rangers.

helps me score because you have to know you can score, and love to score. There is no better feeling than to hear that crowd, or hear the silence when you're visiting."

And Brett will certainly join his father in the Hall.

But the Patricks stand alone as hockey royalty, their three generations of contributions spanning almost the entire history of the Cup.

When the New York Rangers entered the league, the organization hired Lester Patrick to run it, replacing Conn Smythe, who had assembled the roster. In 1928, the club's second season, the Rangers won the Cup with Patrick, the GM/coach, creating one of the most enduring legends in NHL history.

In game two of the final against the Montreal Maroons, Ranger goalie Lorne Chabot was hit by Nels Stewart's shot and rushed to hospital. Since teams didn't carry an extra goalie, and the Maroons wouldn't authorize any of the NHL goalies in the audience to play, Patrick, then 44 years old, donned Chabot's equipment, took a swig of whisky from someone's flask, and went into the net.

When regular Ranger goalie Lorne Chabot went down with an injury during the Stanley Cup final in 1928, head coach Lester Patrick, at the age of 44, donned the pads and backstopped his team to victory, saving 17 of 18 shots.

Muzz Patrick helped the New York Rangers win the Stanley Cup in 1939-40. After heading to Europe to fight in the Second World War, Muzz returned to the NHL in 1945 and played one more season before focusing on coaching.

With dramatic flair—many observers would later report—he stopped 17 of the 18 shots he faced; the Rangers won 2-1. Lester went on to win another Cup, coach 13 seasons, and manage the Rangers for several more.

It was within this aura of hockey celebrity that Muzz and Lynn Patrick were raised. In the early 1930s, Lester sent them both from New York to Quebec, where he'd developed his hockey acumen, to play in Montreal's notoriously competitive City leagues.

Although Lester never considered him a real prospect, he signed Lynn to a $3,500 contract with a $300 signing bonus in 1934. Not sure he'd make the team, Lynn also signed with the Winnipeg Blue Bombers of the Canadian Football League and caught a 68-yard touchdown pass in his limited time there.

But Lynn made the Rangers as a rookie in 1934–35, and so did his younger brother Muzz in 1938. They won the Cup in 1940.

"The fans and the writers didn't take too kindly to the idea of the boss's son moving right into the lineup, especially with no amateur record," Lynn later recalled. "But they accepted me after a while, and I stayed around for ten pretty good seasons."

The best was 1941–42 when he led the league with 32 goals and finished second in NHL overall scoring to linemate Bryan Hextall, the patriarch of the only other three-generation NHL family.

Lynn's son Craig was born in 1946, two months after Lynn's final season as an NHL player, and Craig's brother Glenn, who had a brief NHL career, was born four years later.

"My dreams, when I was young, were to be a player, a coach, and then a manager," said Craig, who sure can pick a fantasy. "I've been able to live my dream, so I'm one of the fortunate people in the world."

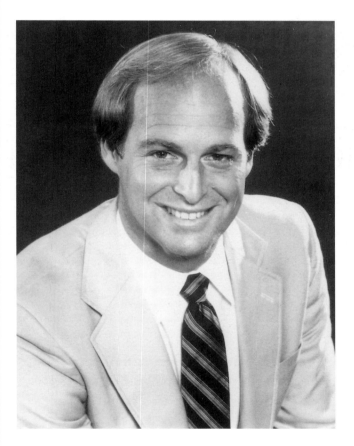

Lynn Patrick, son of Lester and brother of Muzz, enjoyed a Hall of Fame career with the New York Rangers. Lynn retired from active duty in 1947 but was involved in coaching and management with the Rangers, Bruins, and Blues until 1977.

Craig Patrick fulfilled what seemed to be his destiny in 1980 when he was named general manager of the New York Rangers, a position his grandfather Lester had held some 50 years earlier.

At first, the Patricks tried to discourage their son from a career in hockey.

"Doctor or dentist, that's what they kept pushing," Craig said. "But I wasn't going to hear that."

As the Howes used the Olympia as their backyard rink, Craig Patrick learned to skate in the old Boston Garden. His father brought him Terry Sawchuk's

Jiri Bubla joined the Vancouver Canucks at the age of 31. A former member of the Czech national team, he was a solid NHLer, despite entering the league well past his prime.

discarded goaltending equipment, and he and Glenn played ball hockey with it, as Brett Hull had done with Guy Lafleur's stick. And, like the stick, the goalie equipment eventually disintegrated, with the exception of the catching glove, which was later donated to the Hall.

When Craig was 14, the family hockey pilgrimage was repeated as he was sent to Montreal to play in the developmental leagues. A right winger, he was good enough to play for the powerful Montreal Junior Canadiens, and at the University of Denver, his teams won two U.S. college titles. Graduating to the NHL, he scored a modest 72 goals in 401 games for four teams.

In 1979–80, he was assistant GM of the American "Miracle on Ice" team, and in November 1980 he became the youngest (34) GM in Rangers' history, 54 years after his grandfather had accepted the same position.

After almost six years in New York and two as director of athletics at his alma mater in Denver, he coached the Pittsburgh Penguins in 1989, became GM and coach in 1989, and now has two Cups and counting.

"I grew up in the game, and once it's in your blood, it stays in your blood," Craig said.

And that's probably the biggest legacy that NHL veterans bequeath their sons. But is it the genes, or in the environment?

"Genetics," says Jiri Slegr of the Wings, who, like his father, is a defenseman. "To give him credit for me being here, I don't think that would be right. He left home when I was two years old and my step-father, Jozef Slegr, did a good job with me and hockey.

"My mom was a big factor too. She put me in hockey when I was four years old. She was always mentioning that hockey would be a good idea because the genetics would probably show up one

Jiri Slegr's biological father, Jiri Bubla, left home when his son was two years old. Some 20 years later the pair made history as the only father and son to play for the Canucks.

In 1949-50, Max McNab played one of his two seasons in the NHL and managed to get his name on the Stanley Cup, helping the Red Wings defeat the Rangers.

day. And they did. I didn't get to know Jiri Bubla until I was 18."

Slegr has played for five different NHL teams, but his and his father's association with the Canucks is part of a statistical oddity. Although the Canucks were founded in 1970 and are a relatively new franchise, nine of the 69 father-son NHL tandems have Canucks' connections.

Bubla and Slegr are the only father and son to have both played for the Canucks, but Gerry O'Flaherty played there from 1972–78, while his dad, former New York American "Peanuts" O'Flaherty, was chief scout.

Bill McCreary coached the Canucks half a season, from 1973 to 1974, three years after he retired from the NHL. His son Bill Jr. later played 12 NHL games for Toronto. Other sons of NHLers who've played for the Canucks include Mike Walton (Bobby played for Montreal), Ab DeMarco Jr. (Ab Sr. played with four teams), Peter McNab (Dad Max played and managed in the NHL), and Dave Morrison (Jim Morrison played and scouted in the NHL).

Paulin Bordeleau played three years for the early Canucks and his son Sebastien arrived in the NHL in 1995. And Babe Pratt, who won two Cups in a 12-year Hall of Fame career, was the Canucks' special

Although Peter McNab did not win a Stanley Cup like his father Max, he did have an outstanding career, notching 363 goals and 813 points in 954 games.

ambassador when his son Tracy played there from 1973 to 1976.

It can be difficult growing up and playing in the same city where your relative is well-known, as Brian Conacher discovered at various points in his career. His father was Lionel, a member of the Hall, who was selected as Canada's best male athlete of the first half of the 20th century.

So Conacher and his cousin Pete, Charlie's son, bore the weight of double family expectations. But both made it to the NHL, and both spent time with the hometown Leafs, Brian as part of the Leafs' last Cup team in 1967.

After appearing in 95 games with Chicago and the New York Rangers, Emile Francis embarked on his career in management. A Hall of Fame inductee in the Builders category, he acted as coach and/or general manager for the Rangers, Blues, and Whalers.

"I was aware that when I turned professional, it was hard to live up to the legend of Charlie Conacher," Brian said, still playing old-timers' hockey every weekend with Pete.

"Pete was like me. We were journeymen, and being a journeyman Conacher was not enough in the fans' eyes. You realized that no matter how you played, it was not going to be enough.

"It's in the back of your mind that unless you are a star, it isn't enough in people's eyes. I think Wayne Gretzky's kids, for example, might always find that tough. But it wasn't demoralizing for me. I played on a Cup winner. And I didn't feel a lot of pressure growing up, because I was a good athlete."

Bobby Francis had limited success as an NHL player, appearing in only 14 games with the Detroit Red Wings. He followed in father Emile's footsteps and moved behind the bench to coach the Phoenix Coyotes. He was named Coach of the Year in 2001-02.

Brian played two seasons, including the 1964 Olympics, for Father David Bauer's groundbreaking Canadian national team. He also played university hockey and was considered good enough at football to play pro. But he finally joined the Leafs, his uncle's old team, at the age of 25. His two goals against Chicago in the sixth game of the semifinals put the Leafs into the 1967 finals, their last Cup victory.

The coach and GM of that team was Punch Imlach, whose son Brent played three games for the Leafs before turning to college hockey.

Punch's longtime assistant and confidant was the legendary King Clancy, one of the best defenseman of his era in the 1920s and 1930s, a winner of two Cups with Ottawa and one with Toronto. His son Terry eventually made the NHL with the Oakland Seals and the Leafs, and played on the Olympic team with Brian Conacher.

"You heard what your father had done, but you're not trying to emulate them," Clancy says. "Having a famous hockey father was neither a help nor a hindrance, although it's hard at the start. But by the time you turn pro, you already know you can play.

"The one big thing, though, is just being around it. All you hear at the dinner table is hockey."

Dennis Riggin was the son of a goaltender, Melville Riggin, who played senior A hockey when it was nearly as popular as pro hockey. Dennis made it to the NHL for 18 games with Detroit, and his goalie son Pat had a solid ten-year career in the NHL and WHA.

Dennis's younger brother was a junior A goalie, and two of his grandsons are budding netminders. Goaltending doesn't run in this family, it gallops. Even Pat's sister Colleen played net.

"She was pretty intelligent and figured the only way to get attention in our household was to be a goalie or to be the family dog," Dennis laughs. "I

think they played because there was always equipment and sticks lying around the house. Pat never played anything else but goal. Pat hung around with his older brother Larry's friends, and they probably needed a target."

In 1936-37, Syl Apps became the first Maple Leaf to be awarded the Calder Trophy as rookie of the year. He went on to score over 200 goals and win three Stanley Cups in his Hall of Fame career.

Syl Apps is said to be one of the finest men ever to play the game of hockey. When a broken leg shortened his 1942-43 season, he attempted to repay Leaf owner Conn Smythe the money he had been paid in advance for the season.

Pat and Dennis Riggin are the only father and son to each be named the Ontario Hockey League's best goaltender.

Another former Wings' goalie had one of his four sons reach the NHL by bearing down on the net, rather than tending it. Hank Bassen had a 14-year pro career, and played with Chicago, Detroit, and Pittsburgh in the NHL, mostly as a backup. Bob Bassen, though, stayed 15 years in the NHL by being a diligent checker who could play center and left wing.

"At one time all the boys wanted to try goal," said Hank, who raised his family in Calgary. "We always had a little rink in the backyard. One time Mark, the youngest, and his friend talked Bob into using my pads. As soon as they got out there, they ripped one right into his head. All I remember is that Bob came in to take off the pads, and that was that.

"The boys knew I had played. I think it was hard for them, because people look at them and think, 'well if your dad was a pro player, maybe you should be better than you are.'

"Sometimes I wonder if some coaches thought that they didn't want them on the team because their dad played pro. Other coaches, maybe, would think, 'Hey if his dad played hockey, maybe he's got something there.'"

Often the father, knowing the pressures the son will be under anyway, doesn't coach or offer much counsel.

"I only went on the ice twice to help," recalls Denis Brodeur, the father of New Jersey Devils goalie Martin Brodeur.

"And that was to give him some advice about cutting the pass from behind the net to a player in front. But when Martin was going to the local rink for shinny, he'd take his skates on his shoulders and play forward. He only used my stuff for ball hockey, and we caught with different hands."

Denis never played in the NHL, but he did win a bronze medal as a goalie for Canada's 1956 Olympic team. "We used to joke that Martin could not be the best Brodeur until he beat that bronze medal," Denis laughs.

Well, now Martin has met the challenge, playing every game of the medal round as Team Canada won the 2002 Olympic championship.

"It was incredible that we could both win Olympic medals," Martin said. "My own son is only six and he plays goal too. It's exciting to see one of your kids do that.

"Like any dad, mine was a big part of my life. I was playing goalie before I really knew that my dad was a goalie too. I was young enough that I never really caught on.

"But later on, you could see that he was real proud that his son was a goalie too. Like I am, with my son."

In 1975, Syl Apps Jr. became the first son of an all-star player to play in the all-star game himself. Syl Jr. had a very good career tallying 606 points in 727 games.

Old Routes, New Roots

Frank Mahovlich averaged nearly a point per game during his illustrious NHL career and scored over 500 goals during an era when scoring was at a premium.

T HE ROOTS of a tree can often extend in many directions, take many twists, and come out in the strangest places.

So it is with hockey, where bloodlines flow from the ice, behind the benches, to the coach's desk, the front office, the press box, or wrap around a completely different branch of the family. And sadly, like trees, they sometimes are cut down before their time.

Lindy Ruff played and coached the Buffalo Sabres and might have seen brother Brent join him in the NHL one day had tragedy not struck around Christmas 1986. Brent Ruff, then 16, and Swift Current Broncos' teammates Chris Mantyka, Trent Kresse, and Scott Kruger died when the team bus tipped over on a curve of the highway that runs east to Regina, Saskatchewan. The survivors included future Hall-of-Famer Joe Sakic.

Brent, outstanding for his age, was one of four hockey-playing brothers in the Ruff family—Jason was a minor-leaguer who played 14 NHL games, Marty's career ended with a knee injury—and Lindy kept Brent's picture in his coach's office years afterward. Sometimes, when he felt the Sabres' effort was lagging, Lindy would tell Brent's story to the players.

"I think it affected everyone in a positive way," defenseman Jason Woolley would recall. "It really made us step back and think, 'Why am I coming to the rink in such a miserable mood?'

Peter Mahovlich, a two-time all-star, had a pro career that spanned 21 years. He did not score at the rate of brother Frank, but did manage to amass 773 points in 884 NHL games.

"I think [Lindy] told himself after [Brent's death] that he would try to be positive and have some fun when he was at the rink. I just know his brother would be real proud of him now."

At 16, Geoff Courtnall stepped into an important role for 13-year-old younger brother Russ, when their father, Archie, took his own life.

"It hurt us all, but it affected me more than anybody, maybe because of my age," Russ said. "I spent countless nights thinking about it, and I couldn't figure it out. It took me years and years to put it behind me."

The Duncan, B.C., brothers came through the ordeal and played almost 2,000 combined NHL games. Archie had been a good coach to his boys, but had insecurities, which Geoff thought might have been conquered had he known his sons would make it big in the NHL.

"He never got to see us play . . . that's the biggest thing I'm sorry about," Geoff said. "I'm sure if he knew we were going to make it, he'd have tried harder to stick around."

For every serious hockey father who sees his son make the NHL, there are countless others who are disappointed. Most come to grips with it, but Roy Spencer's fanatical devotion to his son Brian's career with the Leafs would come at a terrible price.

On Saturday, December 12, 1970, Roy eagerly tuned in to *Hockey Night in Canada* to see rookie defenseman Brian's first between-periods interview during a game against Chicago.

The family lived in remote Fort St. James, B.C., where Roy had scraped together money for a generator so Brian could get in extra practice on a flood-lit rink. Dying of uremic poisoning, Roy talked all day of seeing *HNIC*'s Ward Cornell talk to his son, a hard-hitting rookie who earned the nickname Spinner.

Geoff Courtnall scored a career high 80 points for the Washington Capitals in 1988-89. He played in the NHL for 17 years, but his career cut short six games into the 1999-2000 season as a result of a vicious open-ice hit.

Russ Courtnall was selected seventh overall by the Maple Leafs in the 1983 entry draft. He went on to play for seven teams, including the Vancouver Canucks, where he teamed up with brother Geoff for 13 games in the 1994-95 season.

Darrin Shannon played 10 seasons in the NHL with the Buffalo Sabres and Winnipeg Jets and Phoenix Coyotes. He played with brother Darryl, for three of his five years with the Jets.

Enraged that the TV station in Prince George had changed to the Vancouver Canucks–California Golden Seals game, Roy drove 90 miles and held the staff at gunpoint, demanding they carry the Leafs and Hawks. Intercepted by the RCMP, he was killed in a gun battle. This incident foreshadowed Brian's own turbulent life and his shooting death in West Palm Beach, Florida, in 1988.

Bill Devorski was a life-long on-ice official with the Ontario Hockey Association, who hoped that among his eight sports-minded children, one might make it to the NHL.

In fact, two sons did, but not as players. Although Bill knew that Paul Devorski was nearing the end of his senior hockey-playing career, he was shocked to read a Toronto paper one day and learn that Paul was retiring to become a referee.

After starting in the rough and tumble world of industrial league hockey, Paul had moved through the junior hockey ranks as a linesman and then refereed in the American Hockey League before joining the NHL in 1989. But Paul wasn't the only son studying the rule books Bill left around their Guelph, Ontario, home. Greg, 11 years Paul's junior, donned a striped shirt after midget hockey and moved up the NHL to become a linesman four years after his brother broke in.

"I grew up not really knowing Paul, because of the gap in our ages, so Dad was the bigger influence on my career," Greg said. "As far as I know, we're the only brothers ever to work in the NHL as officials, but we only do about six games a year together."

Paul refereed and Greg worked the lines for the first time on October 21, 1993, as Detroit beat the Winnipeg Jets 6-2.

"We'll have a pop after the game and talk," Greg said. "Sometimes we'll discuss hockey or [like many

Darryl Shannon was a 2nd round pick of the Maple Leafs but never really found his place in Toronto. He went on to play 544 games over 13 years in the NHL

In a move that sparked much controversy in 1998, Shaun Sutter was drafted in the fourth round by the Calgary Flames when his father, Brian, was head coach.

officials] depending on how that night's game went, we might not talk hockey at all."

Greg was pleased to hear his six-year-old daughter Rachel announce she wanted to follow the family profession after watching her father work a game.

While the Sutter flame will continue to burn in the coaching ranks, eldest brother Brian admitted to being wistful about Ron's retirement in 2001, closing the book on the six-shooter family's playing days.

"But it's funny how it works," Brian said. "Ronny's last year was my son Shaun's first as a pro [in Saint John of the AHL]."

While Shaun's story has yet to be told, and Montreal Canadiens' great Bob Gainey's son Steve is knocking on the door, Darryl Sittler's son Ryan was star-crossed in his efforts to break into the league.

A 1992 Hall of Fame inductee, Bob Gainey won the Conn Smythe Trophy as MVP in 1979's playoffs. He also won the Frank J. Selke Trophy as the League's best defensive player four times.

A first-round draft choice of the Flyers in 1992, the son of the Leafs' icon was compelled to try to live up to the family name, even though he differed in style from Darryl and was dogged by the health problems his father had been able to avoid. But Ryan never played an NHL game, as he was forced to retire after a dangerous facial injury.

"I never pushed him, outside of giving him tips on fitness and things like that," Darryl said. "People

Like Calgary's Brian Sutter, Bob Gainey was criticized after selecting his son Steve in the third round of the 1997 NHL draft.

Hall of Famer Darryl Sittler is best remembered for the magical night in February 1976 when he played against the Boston Bruins and scored six goals and added four assists. His ten points are a single-game record that still stands.

talked about people's expectations of him, but it was about people's expectations of him because of who his dad was.

"It affects him to this day that he didn't play in the NHL and that's something he's had to learn to live with.

"My daughter Meaghan had her share of disappointment, too [the last cut of the 1998 U.S. women's Olympic team, the eventual gold medal winners]. But she's moved on, and Ryan is working as a hockey equipment rep. Like any dad, I just want my kids to be happy."

Broadcaster Dick Irvin would follow his father into the Hall of Fame, yet their paths rarely crossed during the 24 seasons the senior Irvin led the Leafs and later the Montreal Canadiens to 23 playoff appearances, 15 Stanley Cup finals, and four championships.

But the senior Irvin did race back to Calgary the day after the Leafs won the 1932 Cup when he received word his five-week-old namesake was seriously ill with erysipelas, an acute bacterial infection.

"The papers in Toronto were all full of headlines such as 'Irvin might not see new son alive,'" Dick Jr. said.

He recovered, but geography and the demands of the job made it impossible for the family to be together more than once during the season.

"He would leave for training camp at the end of September and usually not be home until April," Irvin said. "We got a little closer to him when we moved to Saskatchewan, but we'd still just come into Montreal for the Christmas holidays."

As Dick Jr. grew older, he was permitted to go on a couple of trips with the team, long train rides with hockey stars that every boy in Canada dreamed of making. There were also the glorious summers

Taken with the seventh overall pick by the Philadelphia Flyers, Ryan Sittler was hoping to follow in the footsteps of his father Darryl. A number of serious injuries, however, have left him on the outside looking in.

191

Chris Drury won the Hobey Baker Award as the top U.S. College player in 1997-98 and in his first season with the Colorado Avalanche, he won the Calder Trophy as rookie of the year.

(following pages) Taken in the second round by the Calgary Flames in 1989, Ted Drury has not managed the same on-ice success as brother Chris. Since graduating from Harvard University, he has appeared in 414 games with seven different teams and scored 41 goals.

when the two Irvins would make up for lost bonding time.

"He would take me to the radio station in Regina," Dick Jr. said. "I remember being fascinated with all the equipment. That's probably where (broadcasting) started for me."

The younger Irvin was not pressured to follow in his dad's footsteps and chose to become an accountant. He moved to Montreal in 1951, not for hockey, but to finish a business degree at McGill University.

But the Forum was a magnet, and soon Irvin was combining both his interests, as a team statistician, a job that continued after his father's death in 1957.

He did dabble in coaching some minor hockey, which prompted new CFCF's TV sports director Brian McFarlane to interview him. Irvin brought along a scrapbook of his father's deeds, and the two future *Hockey Night in Canada* analysts hit it off. For the low-end salary of $75 a week, Irvin launched his TV career.

"I didn't want to come out and just repeat my father's views," Irvin said. "But for years later, something he said would suddenly just come to me in the middle of a broadcast. Then you couldn't shut me up."

Included in the Habs' 12 title seasons Irvin would cover from the booth was the historic March 20, 1971, game between brothers/goaltenders Ken and Dave Dryden.

The rookie Ken wasn't nervous seeing his older sibling warming up at the other end or to spot their dad, Murray, take his seat at the Forum. Coach Al MacNeil told him a couple of days earlier that he would be rested that night and Rogie Vachon would start.

Tony Esposito revolutionized goaltending by introducing the butterfly style – a method employed by many netminders today. He was awarded the Vezina Trophy as top goaltender in his rookie year in 1969-70 and received two more during his career – one in 1971-72 and the other in 1973-74.

(following pages) The Esposito brothers, center Phil and goaltender Tony, both had exceptional NHL careers, culminating in Hall of Fame inductions – Phil in 1984 and Tony in 1988.

"I'd told Dad not to bother coming," Ken said. "But he drove all the way from Toronto anyway."

Dave had carved out a modest living as backup in the NHL, and Ken's natural desire to emulate him had gone from firing pucks and balls at each other outside their Toronto home to taking the same NHL path.

"We were goalies from the very beginning, and he was a huge influence on me," Ken said of Dave. "Even though I was six years younger, he didn't treat me like a punk kid brother. I'd go to his games, he would coach my hockey and baseball teams."

The visiting Sabres posted their lineup first with Dave in net, but when Vachon started, [Buffalo coach] Punch Imlach sent in Joe Daley. Everything was routine, until Vachon went down with an injury early in the second period.

"You always think goalies will get up, but he just stayed there," Ken said. "Eventually, the trainer went out, Rogie was helped off, and Al told me 'you're in.'"

"I knew Imlach was the kind of guy who liked special things to happen. So as soon as he saw me in the crease, he motioned Daley out and my brother in. It was really one of those unbelievable things. Our dad, who took the chance of coming when it made no sense at all, was rewarded."

Montreal was already on its way to a 5-2 win, so the actual duel was irrelevant. But Ken wasn't sure what to do when the game-ending siren sounded, since goalies, even close brothers, weren't supposed to communicate before, during, or after.

"I didn't want any of this attention, and I was trying to get off as quickly as I could," Ken said. "But my brother was smart enough to stand at center and wait. He extended his hand and we shook and a lot of people liked it. But over time, it became too distracting if we played against each other. You wanted your teammates to score, so I didn't enjoy it anymore."

Phil and Tony Esposito were the most famous of the skater/goaltender brother acts, the latest being Mathieu and Martin Biron. But Paul Thompson of the Rangers became the first brother to score on a brother when he beat Cecil (Tiny) Thompson of the Bruins back in the late 1920s.

One of Brian Smith's ten NHL goals came at the expense of older brother Gary "Suitcase" Smith, who played net for seven NHL teams. Brian was a member of the Los Angeles Kings at the time. Gary poignantly retold the story at Brian's funeral in 1995. A popular TV personality in the 1990s, Brian had been shot and killed by a man who had a grudge against the media.

After leaving Irvin in Montreal, McFarlane went to Toronto and began working in TV with Bill Hewitt, son of "He shoots, he scores!" radio pioneer Foster Hewitt. Foster's father William was also involved in hockey and refereed some early Olympic games.

Foster first brought Bill to the Maple Leaf Gardens gondola as a youngster, letting him call the play-by-play once every year on Young Canada Night. Bill made his own name in broadcasting, though the Hewitts wouldn't be the only father-son team.

The late St. Louis Blues' play-by-play man Dan Kelly was followed by sons John (Colorado Avalanche) and Dan Jr. (Columbus Blue Jackets) in the late 1990s. The excitable Ted Darling, who helped put the expansion Sabres on the map, would have been pleased to see son Joel named executive producer of *HNIC* in 2000.

Former *HNIC* producer Ralph Mellanby, who would win fame for his work at the 1988 Olympics, supervised coverage of the 1984 draft in which his son Scott was a second-round pick of the Flyers.

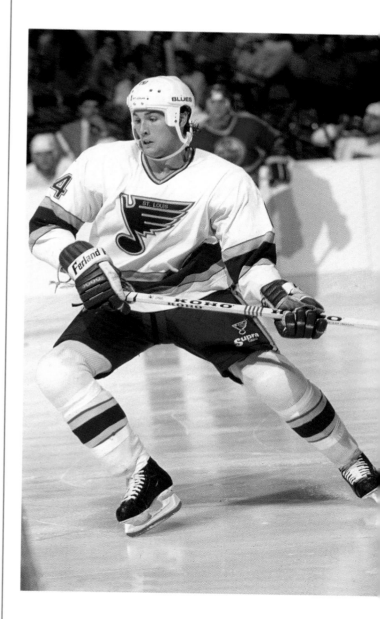

Paul Cavallini shared the ice in St. Louis with brother Gino for five seasons. He toiled with three clubs, the Blues, Capitals, and Stars during his tenure in the NHL.

Gino, the older of the Cavallini brothers, helped the Blues secure play-off berths in all seven of his seasons with the team. A solid two-way player, Gino potted 114 goals during his 593-game career.

Hewitt, Mellanby, the Kellys, and even Irvin, all worked at one time at the Gardens, hockey's most famous building, along with the Montreal Forum. It was home to many families, led by the building's patriarchs, the Smythes.

Ex-soldier Conn Smythe built the place in six months against all odds during the Great Depression, eventually bringing son Stafford into

Scott is the son of former *Hockey Night in Canada* producer Ralph Mellanby. He was taken in the second round of the 1984 draft by the Philadelphia Flyers and has appeared in well over 1,000 games.

John Cullen's career was cut short by a battle with non-Hodgkin's lymphoma. The son of former NHLer Brian Cullen, he was a gifted playmaker, totaling 550 points in 621 career games.

the management of the "Carlton St. Cash Box." But Stafford fell ill and predeceased his father in 1971.

While the Habs had two of the game's most decorated brothers in Rocket and Henri Richard, the Leafs had a number of famous brother/father/son/uncle combinations through the years: the Conachers, Clancys, Cullens, Gardners, Jacksons, and Metzs.

A member of the Morris family was also prominent at the Gardens from opening night in November 1931 to its close in February of 1999. Doug Morris was its first superintendent, responsible for a number of hockey innovations such as the first ice-surfacing equipment, penalty time clocks, and goal lights.

His son Paul's official title was Gardens' sound man (if that was possible when the Beatles and Elvis Presley brought out hordes of screaming girls), but he also helped invent the modern hockey scoreboard. When the regular P.A. man didn't show up for the Leafs' home opener against the Boston Bruins on October 14, 1961, Morris went behind the mike and called more than 1,500 consecutive games, never missing a night until retiring when the Leafs moved to the Air Canada Centre in 1999.

The night the Gardens closed, February 13, 1999, Doug Gilmour was playing for the Chicago Blackhawks, but still received a huge ovation. He had been a Leafs' captain and is one of the top 20 scorers in league history, but it was his father, Don, who helped make him a better player. In a roundabout way, it was also fortunate for Gilmour that older brother Dave washed out in the WHA. During a tour of the Gardens when Dave's Calgary Cowboys visited the Toronto Toros, an awestruck Doug looked around and vowed "some day, I'm going to play here, too."

When Don saw that Dave had hit the wall because his game was not well-rounded, Don switched his

Brothers Dave and Don Maloney were teammates with the New York Rangers from 1978 to 1984.

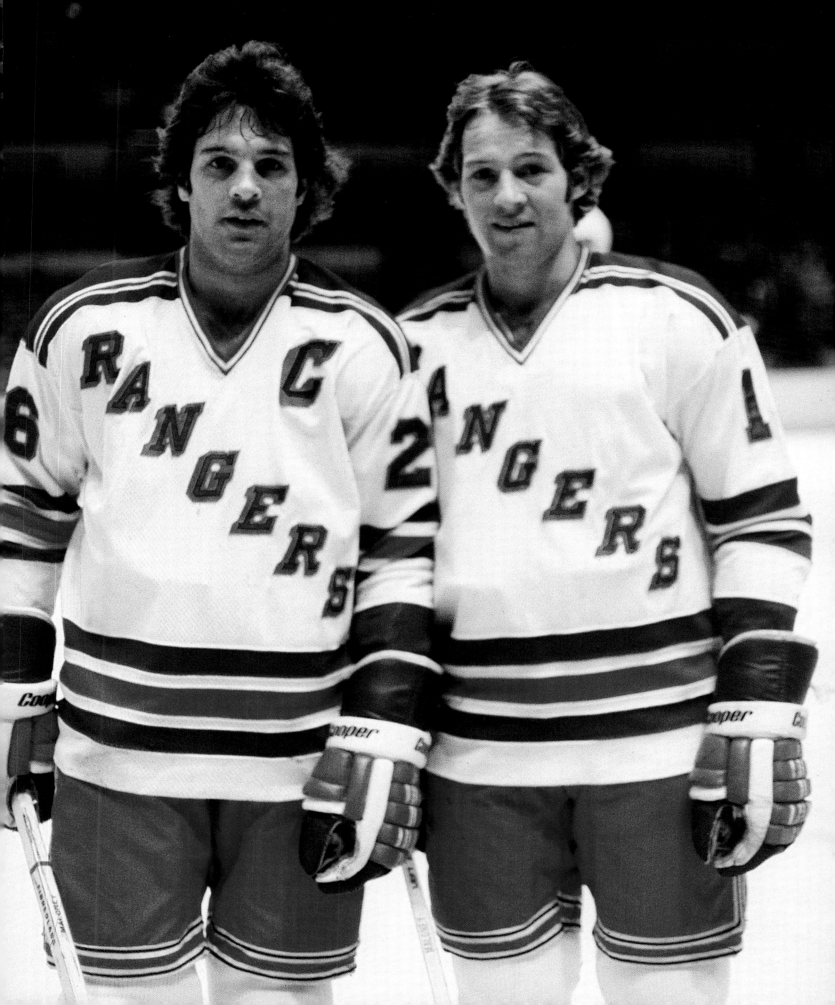

youngest son to defense and put him in a judo class to help his balance. Chosen 134th overall in 1982 because scouts had doubts about his size, Doug Gilmour became one of the game's greatest two-way players and, true to his word, made his mark in Toronto as the club's highest all-time playoff scorer. There was no surrender in this kid, as Dave would later attest.

"I'm 14 years older than Doug, but we'd be playing ball hockey as kids and this little guy would be running me, hacking, and slashing," Dave said. "When we'd play-wrestle, he'd never quit.

"There's a saying he lives by which goes, 'it's not the size of the man, it's what the man does with his size.'"

While Dave got used to being upstaged by his brother, Atlanta Thrashers' forward Pascal Rheaume has dealt with a much different designation.

"I'll always be Manon Rheaume's brother," Pascal said of the only woman to play in an NHL

The Rangers made no mistake when they took Dave Maloney in the first round of the 1974 entry draft. He served as the captain for the better part of three of his 11 seasons with the team.

Don, the younger of the hockey-playing Maloney brothers, was a second-round draft choice of the New York Rangers in 1978. He spent the bulk of his 765 games with the team before a trade during the 1988-89 season sent him to the Hartford Whalers. He finished his career with the Islanders.

Doug Gilmour arrived in Toronto thanks to a trade from the Calgary Flames
mid-way through the 1991-92 season. He went on to play five seasons for the
Leafs and in 1993, brought them within one game of the Stanley Cup finals.

Pascal will always be the lesser known of the hockey-playing Rheaume children, despite the fact his sibling never played an NHL regular season game.

On September 23, 1992, Manon Rheaume made hockey history
with the expansion Tampa Bay Lightning, as the first woman
to appear in an NHL exhibition game.

game. "But that's okay. She deserves the recognition. I'm really proud of all that she's accomplished."

Manon played goal for the Tampa Bay Lightning against St. Louis in an exhibition game in 1992, allowing two goals in 20 minutes. She and Pascal also played a game for the Quebec Major Junior Hockey League Sherbrooke Castors.

"She was the backup, but we were down 6-1, and Jocelyn Thibault got pulled and she went in," Pascal said. "I was really nervous for her, but she did a great job."

Manon cut back her ice time after helping Canada to a silver medal at the 1998 Olympics, but she stays in constant contact with Pascal, encouraging his career.

The diminutive Tony Granato was drafted by the New York Rangers in 1982 but did not make his NHL debut until 1988. He went on to play over 700 games and was awarded the Bill Masterton Trophy in 1997 after coming back from a near fatal head injury.

Tony Granato, who played almost 800 NHL games, gave similar support to younger sister Cammi, one of the best female players the United States has ever produced. The two Chicago suburbanites have both represented their countries at the Olympics.

While Mark Howe and Brett Hull thrived after their famous fathers retired, Eric Lacroix had to play under a different type of pressure. His dad, Pierre

The most decorated women's hockey player ever, Cammi Granato led the United States to the gold medal at the 1998 Olympics in Nagano, Japan. She was also named U.S. Women's College player of the year three times.

Lacroix, was a player agent and later GM of the Colorado Avalanche. Eric earned his way to the NHL, despite the inevitable whispers of nepotism during his three seasons with the Avs.

The Hextalls and Patricks weren't the only families to have grandfathers and grandsons make an impact.

St. Louis Blues' goaltender Brent Johnson was the grandson of Red Wings' Production Line forward Sid Abel. His father, Bob, also played goal for St. Louis and Pittsburgh. Scott Pellerin of the Dallas Stars is the grandson of Irish immigrant Sammy McManus, who was a fine amateur and made it to the NHL long enough to win a Cup with the Montreal Maroons in 1935.

U.S. gold medal Olympian and NHLer Dave Silk's grandfather, Hal Janvrin, wasn't a hockey player, but he did win a World Series as a second baseman with the Boston Red Sox.

Dit Clapper, whose No. 5 was retired by the Boston Bruins, had a grandson, Greg Theberge,

Brent Johnson, the grandson of Sid Abel, earned the starting job in St. Louis after posting 19 wins in his 31 starts as a rookie.

named best defenseman in the Ontario Hockey League in 1979. He was later an AHL all-star and played 153 games for the Washington Capitals.

Many other great hockey families were brought together through holy matrimony. Had he lived, Morenz would have become father-in-law to Bernie "Boom Boom" Geoffrion, whose own daughter married NHLer Hartland Monahan. Bernie's son Danny started in the league about the same time Hartland's brother Garry was finishing.

Bernie "Boom Boom" Geoffrion played 16 seasons in the NHL, winning the Calder, Art Ross, and Hart Trophies during his storied career. He was a member of the Canadiens during their run of five consecutive Stanley Cups from 1956-60.

Valeri Vasiliev, eight-time world champion for the former Soviet Union, became a father-in-law to Alexei Zhamnov, now of the Blackhawks. Hawks' senior vice-president Bob Pulford is father-in-law to San Jose Sharks GM Dean Lombardi. Chicago Blackhawks' forward Peter White married Jody Clarke, the daughter of Philadelphia Flyers' boss Bob Clarke.

Danny, the son of former Montreal Canadien "Boom Boom" Geoffrion, was a star at the junior level but never found his place in the NHL. He played 111 games with Winnipeg and Montreal, scoring 20 goals. His final season as a pro was spent with the Yukijrushi Sopporo of the Japanese Professional League.

The Chicago Blackhawks traded away Phil Esposito following the 1966-67 season. He went on to become one of the greatest players in the history of the game, and after retirement, was responsible for bringing the NHL to the state of Florida. He was the general manager of the Lightning from 1992 to 1998.

For a while, Alexander Selivanov's nickname in Tampa Bay was "Son-in-Law-of" after he tied the knot with Lightning chief Phil Esposito's daughter Carrie.

Bobby Holik's sister, tennis star Andrea Holikova, married fellow Czech Frank Musil. Goalie Al Smith wed Nancy Keon, a cousin of one-time Leafs' teammate Dave. Former Sabre, Red Wing, and Leaf Mike Foligno married the niece of Rangers' goaltending great Ed Giacomin, and Mike Murphy met wife Yvon through L.A. Kings' teammate Vic Venasky, whose wife and Yvon were sisters. Murphy's son Patrick was drafted by Edmonton in 2002.

Brothers-in-law Shayne Corson and Darcy Tucker are on the same Leafs' team, the same line, and do some commercial ventures together as the "Bruise Brothers." Tucker was first introduced to Corson's sister Shannon when both played for the Canadiens; Corson later followed Tucker to the Leafs as a free agent in 2000.

Corson leaned heavily on Tucker early in the 2000–01 season when he suffered a series of panic attacks that sometimes required Tucker to talk him through the night at visiting hotels or on the bench during a game.

But in-laws haven't always been seen in such a positive light. Former Leafs' coach Tom Watt was in a fit of rage one night after a loss to Calgary, which he blamed in part on the fact that Calgary's coach Doug Risebrough was referee Terry Gregson's brother-in-law.

Cousins are spread far and wide as well. When the 1998 expansion Nashville Predators first lined up against the Phoenix Coyotes, respective captains Tom Fitzgerald and Keith Tkachuk re-lived some New England memories. Jeff Beukeboom and Joe Nieuwendyk were a pair of tough customers, whose

After an exceptional junior career, Darcy Tucker took some time adjusting to the NHL game. He seems to have found his pro legs and set career highs with 24 goals and 59 points in 2001-02.

Shayne Corson was a first-round draft choice of the Montreal Canadiens and has never played a game in the minors. The consummate team player, he has served as captain for both the St. Louis Blues and Edmonton Oilers.

uncle was Dutch-born defenseman Ed Kea. When Tod Sloan ended his two-Cup NHL career in Chicago in 1960–61, he welcomed young cousin Dave Keon to the Toronto fold.

Two of the most decorated cousins of all time are Ron Francis, still setting league-scoring milestones with the Carolina Hurricanes and goaltender Mike Liut, a Hart Trophy finalist to Gretzky in 1981.

With the exception of Gretzky's brother Brent, the Edmonton Oilers dynasty didn't reproduce itself, although Mark Messier's brother, Paul, played nine games for Colorado in 1978–79 and his cousins Joby and Mitch played a combined 45 NHL games. Messier's brother-in-law is ex-Bruin John Blum.

John Kordic, an Edmonton, Alberta native was plagued by off-ice problems throughout his seven-year career. His well-documented battle with drugs and alcohol finally took its toll when he died of cardiac arrest in a Quebec City hotel room in 1992.

Wendel Clark arrived in Toronto as the first overall pick in 1985 and did not disappoint. His rugged style of play soon made him a fan favorite and he was named captain of the team prior to the 1991 season. He still remains one of the most popular players to ever wear the blue and white.

In two memorably rough playoff series between the Leafs and Wings in the late 1980s, the media made much of Kelvington, Saskatchewan, "cousins" Wendel Clark and Joey Kocur playing each other but refusing to fight.

Fifteen years later, Wings' video coach Kocur was still trying to set the record straight.

"Wendel and I are somehow related by marriage on his grandfather's side, but the connection is so distant I have no idea what it is," Kocur said. "Wendel might have said to the media we were first cousins or something and it spread everywhere. Rather than go to every reporter and explain, we just said nothing. If you go far enough back in Kelvington, you'll find everyone is probably related somehow.

"As far as us not fighting, we didn't because he was a scorer, and there was no reason for him to bother with someone like me."

Also mistaken as cousins of Clark and Kocur at various times were future Los Angeles Kings' coach Barry Melrose and St. Louis Blues' tough guy Kelly Chase.

"Barry's brother married my first cousin, so at least he's in sight," Kocur said. "But Kelly was just a neighbor from Porcupine Plain, a Kelvington wannabe."

There are many more wrongful assumptions of relations, particularly when common surnames such as Smith and Brown come into play, and you have to separate the Johnsons from the Johnstons and the Jonssons.

Total Hockey listed nine Lemieuxs having played in the modern era and in 1986–87, which included two sets of brothers Mario and Alain, and Claude and Jocelyn.

Many believed Adam Deadmarsh of the Kings was Butch's son, but the Trail, B.C., boys are actually

Destined for greatness since his days in junior hockey, Mario Lemieux has averaged nearly two points per game during his outstanding career.

Alain Lemieux appeared in 119 games during his ten-year hockey career, including one game alongside brother Mario as a member of the Pittsburgh Penguins.

Known for their feisty style of play, the Lemieux brothers Claude and Jocelyn have collectively appeared in over 1,700 games.

second cousins; same with defensemen Darren and the older Ed Van Impe of Saskatoon, Saskatchewan. Nor were Darcy and Randy Rota brothers, but cousins, as are current NHLers Joe and Scott Thornton.

Fred and Henry Harris also shared an unusual bond and not only because both were Bruins (Fred in 1924–5 and Henry in 1930–31). Both were also known as "Smokey," which for years caused headaches for historians bent on proving they weren't the same person.

The New Jersey Devils won just 17 games during the 1983–84 campaign, and critics blamed it on little-brother syndrome, insisting the Devils suited up the wrong Broten (Aaron), Larmer (Jeff), and Trottier (Rocky). All three of their older siblings— Neal Broten, Steve Larmer, and Bryan Trottier—were NHL stars at the time.

The Leafs traded away Doug Jarvis before he embarked on the NHL's longest consecutive game streak and won four Cups with Montreal, but signed

(opposite) Claude Lemieux has won four Stanley Cups, two with New Jersey and one with both Montreal and Colorado. His first Cup with the Devils in 1994-95 came with a bonus prize: he was awarded the Conn Smythe Trophy as playoff MVP.

Jocelyn Lemieux's best NHL campaign was in 1992–93 as a member of the Chicago Blackhawks. He scored ten goals and added 21 assists.

his significantly lesser-known cousin Wes a few years later.

Distant cousins and future Washington Capital teammates Al Iafrate and Dino Ciccarelli wound up on the American and Canadian sides of the Detroit River, while Pat Quinn coached distant cousin Adam Mair when both joined the Leafs in 1998.

After a successful career as an NHL defenceman, Pat Quinn first moved behind the bench during the 1978–79 season with the Philadelphia Flyers. He has gone on to coach in Los Angeles, Vancouver, and Toronto.

Maple Leaf coach and general manager Pat Quinn did not play favorites with distant cousin Adam Mair. He traded the right winger to the L.A. Kings in a move that brought Aki Berg to Toronto.

Kelly Miller, the eldest of three brothers who played in the NHL, appeared in 1,057 games as a Washington Capital and New York Ranger.

In the past few years, fathers, sons, and brothers have begun to pop up in management and player representation. Phoenix Coyotes' exec Cliff Fletcher, GM in Calgary and Toronto, influenced son Chuck, who worked for player rep giant Newport Sports before joining the Florida Panthers management team. Jason Arnott's brother Wade is with Newport as well.

The Fletchers briefly became father-son rivals in the 2001–02 season when Chuck was made interim GM in Florida.

"It's great experience for him," the elder Fletcher said. "Assuming that role, even on a temporary basis, will give him a little baptism of what it's like to make decisions instead of just offering advice."

Glen Sather, who had little time for agents when he ran the cash-strapped Edmonton Oilers, was taken aback when son Justin considered joining that profession. But he tried to be supportive.

Despite being a tenth-round pick of the New York Rangers, Kevin Miller played 616 NHL games.

"Hockey is all we ever did know in our family," Glen Sather said. "It's a great sport, with lots of opportunity, no matter what you want to do."

For the Allison brothers, that is symbolized in a picture each holds dear from the 1983–84 season.

Mike was out of the New York Rangers' lineup that night with a shoulder injury, rotten luck as Dave came to town for one of his three career appearances for the Canadiens in his otherwise mundane minor league career. But it was a moment too special to waste.

"You've got to skate with me in the warm-up," Dave begged Mike.

Using borrowed equipment, Mike did exactly that, and long after the other players had gone to the dressing room, the joyous brothers from Fort Frances, Ontario, stayed out on the ice while a friend snapped away with a camera.

"If the road to success is a journey, mine's been a rocky one," Dave said. "But I'm proud of my brother. I know how much you have to sacrifice to get there."

Whether it's ten years, or in the case of the Allisons, barely ten minutes, the time spent with a relative in hockey's greatest theater is to be cherished.

When the hair grays and the goals, assists, and dressing-room banter fade to distant memory and the odd dog-eared photo, the hockey family will endure.

Kip Miller kept with family tradition and played college hockey at Michigan State University as brothers Kevin and Kelly had before him. He was the highest drafted of the Millers, going 72nd overall to the Quebec Nordiques.

The Families

Brothers
Twins
Three Brothers
Four Brothers
Six Brothers
Executives
Coaches and Scouts
Officials and Players
Players and Trainers
Owners and Scouts
Agents and Players
Brothers and Sisters
Fathers and Sons
Players and Executives
GMs and Coaches
Executives
Scouts
Trainers and Players
Fathers and Daughters
Coaches and Broadcasters
Broadcasters
Grandfathers and Grandsons
Fathers-in-Law and Sons-in-Law
Brothers-in-Law
Uncles and Nephews
Cousins

BROTHERS

Thommy and Christer
    Abrahamsson
Jack and Bill Adams
George and Viv Allen
Dave and Mike Allison
Ernie and Jocko Anderson
Mikail and Niklas Andersson
John and Ty Arbour
Wayne and Dave Babych
Fred and John Barrett
Andy and Frank Bathgate
Joe and Gordie Bell

Jim and Brian Benning
Max and Doug Bentley
Doug and Ken Berry
Mathieu and Martin Biron
Chuck and George Blair
Conrad and Jean Bourcier
Ken and Len Broderick
Doug and Greg Brown
Jeff and Jack Brownschidle
Eddie and Mud Bruneteau
Glenn and Gord Brydson
Pavel and Valeri Bure
Ron and Mike Busniuk

Yuri and Vacheslav Butsayev	*Bill and Bun Cook*	Wayne and Gary Dillon
Jack and Terry Caffery	Lloyd and Leo Cook	*Marcel and Gilbert Dionne*
Drew and Jock Callendar	Bert and Con Corbeau	Pat and Pete Donnelly
James and Tony Camazolla	Les and Murray Costello	Ted and Chris Drury
Jack and David Capuano	Sylvain and Alain Cote	Ken and Dave Dryden
Jack and Steve Carlson	Art and Tommy Coulter	Murray and Mike Eaves
Bob and Bill Carse	Yvan and Norm Cournoyer	*Phil and Tony Esposito*
Gino and Paul Cavallini	*Geoff and Russ Courtnall*	Sergei and Fedor Fedorov
Don and Dick Cherry	Keith and Bruce Crowder	Peter and Chris Ferraro
Sprague and Odie Cleghorn	Nick and Hank Damore	Bob and Marcel Fillion
Dan and Sylvain Cloutier	Harold and Jack Darragh	Ed and Frank Finnigan
Mac and Neil Colville	Shirley and Cam Davidson	Rod and Magnus Flett
Mike and Paul Comrie	Cy and Corb Denneny	Ron and Bob Flockhart

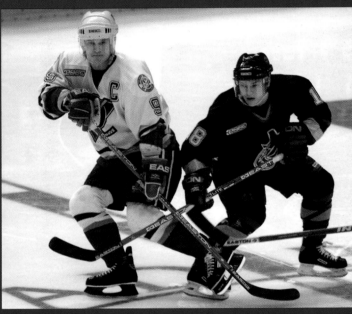

Archie and Harry Fraser	Ossie and Emil Hanson
Paul and Dave Gardner	Todd and Brett Harkins
Bob and Brad Gassoff	Fred and Henry Harris
Brian and Gerry Gibbons	Kevin and Darien Hatcher
Mike and Paul Gillis	Andy and Clay Hebenton
Doug and Dave Gilmour	Bryan Jr. and Dennis Hextall
Fred and Howie Glover	Wally and Phil Hergesheimer
John and Larry Gould	Pat and Greg Hickey
Gilles and Norm Gratton	Bill and Ernie Hicke
Red and Shorty Green	Glenn and Doug Hicks
Mark and Bruce Greig	Ed and Cecil Hoekstra
Wayne and Brent Gretzky	Gary and Randy Holt
Jean and Gilles Hamel	Marian and Marcel Hossa

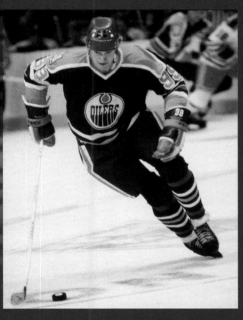

Gordie and Vic Howe	Paul and Steve Kariya	*Claude and Jocelyn Lemieux*
Marty and Mark Howe	Forbes and Jamie Kennedy	Pit and Hec Lepine
Harry and Ron Howell	Mike and Bill Kitchen	Trevor and Jamie Linden
Bobby and Dennis Hull	John and Dan Kordic	*Eric and Brett Lindros*
Peter and Miroslav Ihnacak	Arnie and Eddie Kullman	Hakan and Peter Loob
Busher and Art Jackson	Bill and Gus Kyle	Clem and Wilf Loughlin
Joe and Frank Jerwa	Bob and Mark LaForest	Gerry and Fred Lowrey
Greg and Ryan Johnson	Dave and Scott Langkow	Billy and Bob MacMillan
Aurel and Rene Joliat	Steve and Jeff Larmer	*Frank and Peter Mahovlich*
Bob and Jim Jones	Stephan and Patrick Lebeau	Wayne and Chico Maki
Kenny and Jorgen Jonsson	Greg and Brad Leeb	Joe and Jeff Malone
Tomas and Frantisek Kaberle	Chuck and Bryan Lefley	Dave and Don Maloney
Gord and Sheldon Kannagiesser	Mario and Alain Lemieux	Randy and Kris Manery

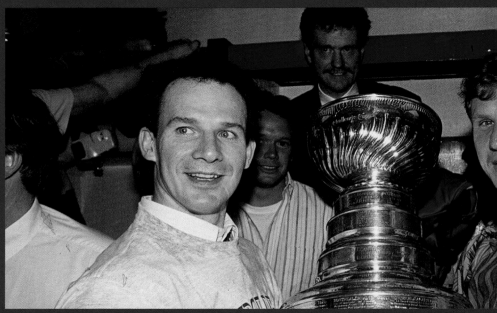

Sylvio and Georges Mantha	Mark and Paul Messier
Ted and Bob McAneeley	Don and Nick Metz
Norm and Jud McAtee	Art and John Michaluk
Keith and Bill McCreary	Joe and Pat Micheletti
Brian and Darwin McCutcheon	Bob and Paul Miller
Hartland and Bob McDougall	*Boris and Dmitri Mironov*
Basil and Chris McRae	Don and Jim McLeod
Marty and Chris McSorley	John and Carl Mokosak
Harry and Gordon Meeking	Mike and Randy Moller
Dick and Barry Meissner	Gary and Hartland Monahan
Gilles and Denis Meloche	Mark and Doug Morrison
Howie and Hillary Menard	Rod and Don Morrison
Jody and Mitch Messier	Kenny and Wayne Mosdell

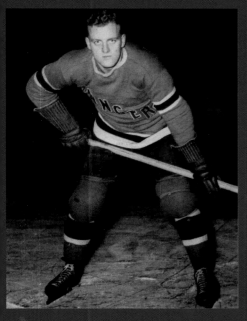
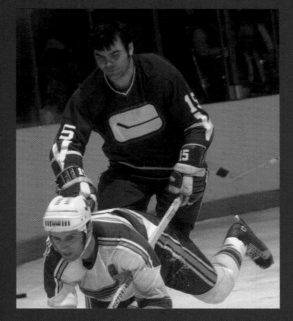
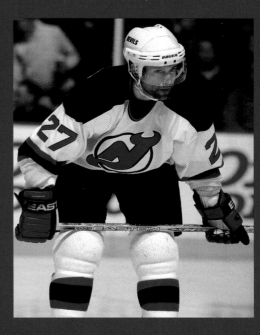

Joe and Brian Mullen

Grant and Paul Mulvey

Don and Bob Murdoch

Jeff and Todd Nelson

Jeff and Kirk Nielson

Rob and Scott Niedermayer

Eddie and Russ Oatman

Mike and Tim O'Connell

Lyle and Selmar Odelein

Kevin and Danny O'Shea

Rosaire and Wilf Paiement

Bob and Dick Paradise

Larry and Doug Patey

James and Steve Patrick

Muzz and Lynn Patrick

Craig and Glenn Patrick

Gord and Eric Pettinger

Roger and Noel Picard

Larry and Jim Playfair

Rob and Ron Plumb

Don and Bud Poile

Paul and Jan Popeil

Denis and Jean Potvin

Dean and Eric Prentice

Keith and Wayne Primeau

Chris and Sean Pronger

Bill and Max Quakenbush

Ken and Terry Reardon

Mickey and Dick Redmond

Robert and Martin Reichel

Maurice and Henri Richard

Shawn and Jamie Rivers

Mario and Serge Roberge

Larry and Moe Robinson

Torrie and Gordie Robertson

Doug and Gordie Roberts

Earl and Michel Roche

Brian and Greg Rolston

Doug and Lorne Rombough

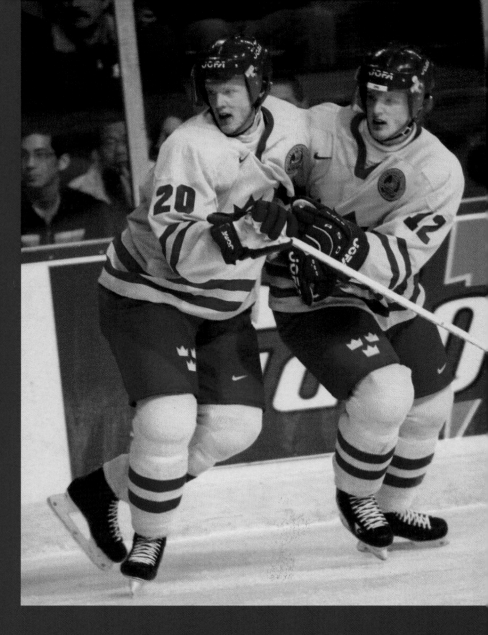

236

Patrick and Stephane Roy

Lindy and Jason Ruff

Bob and Gary Sabourin

David and Joe Sacco

J.F. and Bob Sauve

Bobby and Cliff Schmautz

Joe and Jackie Schmidt

Ron and Danny Schock

Daniel and Hendrik Sedin

Rod and Ric Seiling

Gerry and Charles Shannon

Darrin and Darryl Shannon

Johnny and Frank Sheppard

Jack and Bill Shill

Darryl and Gary Sittler

Tim and Neil Sheehy

Steve and Byron Shutt

Paul and John Shymr

Cully and Thain Simon

Gary and Brian Smith

Kenny and Don A. Smith

Des and Roger Smith

Carl and Dalton Smith

Billy and Gord Smith

Kevin and Ryan Smyth

Gene and Dennis Sobchuk

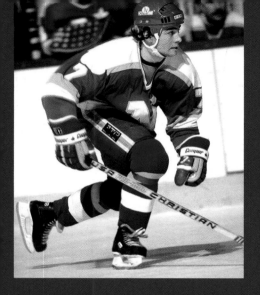

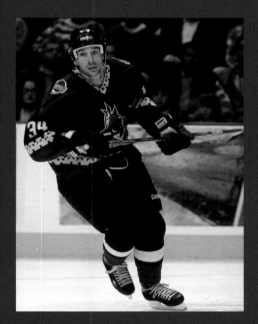

Edward and Myron Stankiewicz
Scott and Mike Stevens
Hod and Bruce Stuart
Frank and Peter Sullivan
Tim and Chris Taylor
Skip and Skeeter Teal
Tiny and Paul Thompson
Jerry and Zellio Toppazzini
Bryan and Rocky Trottier
Pierre and Sylvain Turgeon
Jan and Roman Vopat
Grant and Bill Warwick
Joe and Jim Watson

Don and Chick Webster
Blake and Glen Wesley
Gord and Fred Williams
Tom and Warren Williams
Larry and Johnny Wilson
Murray and Doug Wilson
Ken and Gary Yaremchuk

TWINS
Chris and Peter Ferraro
Joel and Henrik Lundquist
Henrik and Daniel Sedin

Ron and Rich Sutter
Peter and Patrik Sundstrom

THREE BROTHERS
Doug, Max, and Reg Bentley
Curt, Harvey Jr., and Bill Bennett
J.P., Paulin, and Christian Bordeleau
Neal, Aaron, and Paul Broten
Jack, Steve, and Jeff Carlson
Bill, Jerry, and Frank Carson
Charlie, Lionel, and Roy Conacher
Bill, Bun, and Bud Cook
Bob, Marc, and Lou Crawford

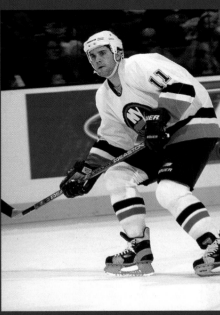

Brian, Barry, and Ray Cullen

Kevin, Gord, and Peter Dineen

Paul, Doug, and Kevin Evans

Pat, Gordie, and Ray Hannigan

Dave, Suddy, and Billy Gilmour

Kevin, Derian, and Mark Hatcher

Larry, Wayne, and Floyd Hillman

Mark, Dale, and Dave Hunter

Wally, Hec, and Ken Kilrea

Tony, Peter, and Jack Leswick

Kelly, Kevin, and Kip Miller

Bill, Barclay, and Bob Plager

Chubby, Rocket, and Joe Power

Marcel, Jean, and Claude Pronovost

Bobby, Roland, and Guy Rousseau

Alf, Harry, and Tommy Smith

Fred, Jack, and Jim Stanfield

Peter, Marian, and Anton Stastny

FOUR BROTHERS

Frank, George, Bobby, and
　Billy Boucher

Harvey Jr., Curt, Bill, and
　John Bennett

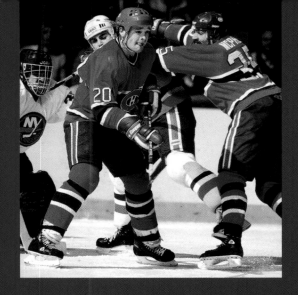 

SIX BROTHERS
Brian, Darryl, Duane, Brent, Rich
  and Ron Sutter

EXECUTIVES
Craig and Todd Button
George and Gordon Gund
Jeremy and Louis Jacobs
Seymour and Northrup Knox

COACHES AND SCOUTS
Frank and Dick Carroll
Marc and Lou Crawford

Fred and Sandy Hucul
Bryan and Terry Murray
Scott and Jack Bowman
Bob and Mark Johnson

OFFICIALS AND PLAYERS
Joe and Gil Nieuwendyk
Andy and Bruce Van Hellemond
Jim and Mick McGeough
Glen and Art Skov

PLAYERS AND TRAINERS
Kevin and Ken Lowe

OWNERS AND SCOUTS
Wayne and Keith Gretzky

AGENTS AND PLAYERS
Gerry and Herb Pinder

BROTHERS AND SISTERS
Tony and Cammi Granato
Pascal and Manon Rheaume

FATHERS AND SONS
Syd and Gerry Abel
Syl Apps Jr. and Sr.

Ron and Bob Atwell

Hank and Bob Bassen

Harvey Bennett Jr. and Sr.

Bill and Curt Bennett

Rene and Mark Boileau

Paulin and Sebastien Bordeleau

Butch and Pierre Bouchard

Scott and Steve Bowman

Adam and Andy Brown

Jiri Bubla and Jiri Slegr

Bucky and Ron Buchanan

Colin and Gregory Campbell

Red and Gene Carr

Guy and Eric Chouinard

King and Terry Clancy

Lionel and Brian Conacher

Charlie and Pete Conacher

Dave and Adam Creighton

Barry and John Cullen

Ab DeMarco Jr. and Sr.

Bill and Kevin, Gord and Peter
  Dineen

Norm and Christian Dube

Norm and Craig Ferguson

Lidio and Lee Fogolin Sr. and Jr.

Kent and Peter Forsberg

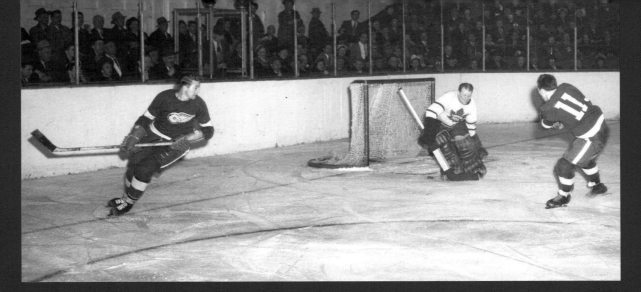

Emile and Bobby Francis
Bob and Steve Gainey
Cal and Dave, Paul Gardner
Bernie and Danny Geoffrion
Hank and Glenn Goldup
Ron and John Grahame
Matti and Niklas Hagman
Ted and Gord Hampson
Bill and Chris Hajt
Gord and Alan Haworth
Murray and Dany Heatley
Bryan and Bryan Jr., Dennis
   Hextall

Bryan Jr. and Ron Hextall
Wayne and Alex Hicks
Ken Hodge Sr. and Jr.
Jaroslav and Bobby Holik
Lou and Chuck Holmes
Gordie and Mark, and Marty Howe
Harry and Ron Howell
Bobby and Brett Hull
Earl Ingarfield Sr. and Jr.
Bill and Trevor Johansen
Bob and Brent Johnson
Frantisek and Frantisek Jr., Tomas
   Kaberle

Bob and Chad Kilger
Roger and Jason Lafreniere
Jacques and Daniel Laperriere
Claude and Guy Larose
Reggie and Jamie Leach
Barry and Randy Legge
Bert and Ted Lindsay
Sam and Peter Lopresti
Jack and Fleming Mackell
John and Wes McCauley
Bill and Bill E. McCreary
Mike and Mike W. McMahon
Max and Peter, David McNab

Gilles and Eric Meloche

Jim and Dave Morrison

Mike and Patrick Murray

Bob and Eric Nystrom

Peanuts and Gerry O'Flaherty

Aldo and Doug Palazzari

Lester and Muzz, Lynn Patrick

Lynn and Craig, Glenn Patrick

Jim and Jimmy Peters

Babe and Tracy Pratt

Nelson and Taylor Pyatt

Clare and Herb Raglan

Leo Reise Sr. and Jr.

Dennis and Pat Riggin

Doug and David Roberts

Doug and Bob Robinson

Oliver and Earl Seibert

Darryl and Ryan Sittler

Thomas and Alexander Steen

Des and Brian, Gary Smith

Stu E. and Brian Smith

Stan and John Smrke

Pat and Mike Stapleton

Nick and Rogie Vachon

Bob and Mike Walton

Don and Joe Ward

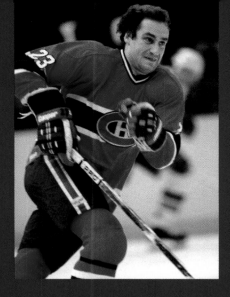

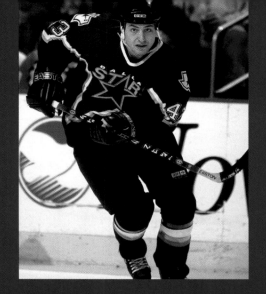

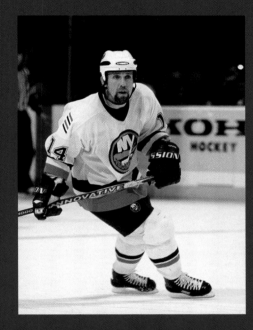

Harry (Rat) and Tommy Westwick.
Larry and Ron Wilson
Jerry and Carey Wilson
Rik and Landon Wilson

PLAYERS AND EXECUTIVES
Max and Peter McNab
Pierre and Eric Lacroix

GMS AND COACHES
Cliff and Chuck Fletcher
Emile and Bob Francis
Bob and Steve Gainey

Punch and Brent Imlach
Bobby and Richard Kromm
Jacques and Daniel Laperriere
Lou and Marty Nanne
Fred and Ray Shero

EXECUTIVES
John Ferguson Sr. and Jr.
Mike, Marrion, Chris, and
    Denise Illich
Peter and Jason Karmanos
Pierre and Eric Lacroix
John H. and John P. McConnell

Max and Peter McNab
George and Paul McNamara
James and Bruce Norris
Bud and David Poile
John and Tim, Michael and
    James Regis
Conn and Stafford Smythe
Ed and Jay Snider
Bill and Peter, Michael Wirtz

OFFICIALS
Charlie and David Banfield
John and Angelo D'Amico

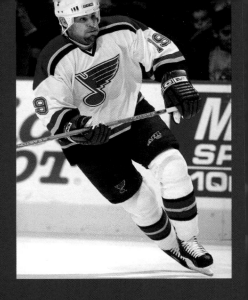

Paul and Greg Devorski
Kerry and Ryan Fraser
Don and Jamie Koharski
Bill and Mike McCreary
Bill and Paul Stewart

SCOUTS
Pierre Dorion Sr. and Jr.
Don and Scott Luce
Clint and Garth Malarchuk
Joe and Mark Yannetti

TRAINERS/PLAYERS
Cal and Jason and Jennifer Botterill
Carey and Gerry Wilson

FATHERS AND DAUGHTERS
Darryl and Meaghan Sittler

COACHES AND BROADCASTERS
Dick Irvin, Jr. and Sr.

BROADCASTERS
Ted and Joel Darling
Bill and Foster Hewitt

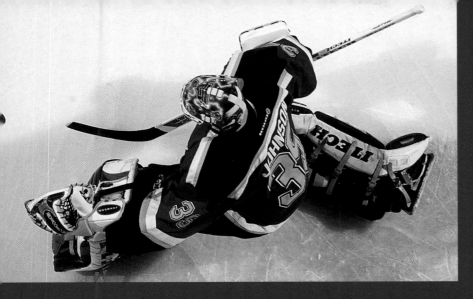

Dan and Dan Jr. and John Kelly
Ralph and Scott Mellanby

GRANDFATHERS AND GRANDSONS

Sid Abel and Brent Johnson
Dit Clapper and Greg Theberge
Bryan Hextall Sr. and Ron Hextall
Howie Morenz and Danny
  Geoffrion
Sammy McManus and Scott
  Pellerin
Lester Patrick and Glenn Patrick

Lester Patrick and Craig Patrick
Jean Pusie and P.C. Drouin
Bill and Paul Stewart
Cyclone and Mark Taylor

FATHERS-IN-LAW AND SONS-IN-LAW

Sid Abel and Bob Johnson
Clarence Campbell and Garry
  Monahan
Bobby Clarke and Peter White
Phil Esposito and Alexander
  Selivanov

Bernie Geoffrion and Hartland
  Monahan
Howie Menard and Darren Eliot
Howie Morenz and Bernie
  Geoffrion
George Swarbrick and Greg Adams
Bob Pulford and Dean Lombardi.

BROTHERS-IN-LAW

Alain Cote and Luc Dufour
Danny Geoffrion and Hartland
  Monahan
Bobby Holik and Frank Musil

246

Harry Howell and Ron Murphy	Darcy Tucker and Shayne Corson
Rick Lapointe and Brad Maxwell	
Don Lever and Rick Ley	UNCLES AND NEPHEWS
Don Luce and Mike A. Boland	Ray and Rick Adduono
Mark Messier and John Blum	George Armstrong and Dale and
Mike Murphy and Vic Venasky	Dan McCourt
Mark Napier and Pat Hughes	Larry Aurie and Cummy Burton
Mike Posavad and Kerry Huffman	Christian, J.P. and Sebastien
Doug Risebrough and Terry	Bordeleau
Gregson	*Charlie and Roy Conacher; Pete and*
Wayne Rutledge and Dale Rolfe	*Brian Conacher*
Larry Sacharuk and Greg Holst	Roy and Don Edwards
Al Smith and Dave Keon	Charlie, Roy, and Lionel Conacher

247

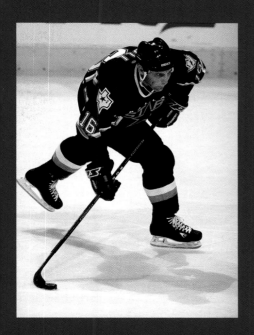

and Murray Henderson	Peanuts O'Flaherty and Craig	Barney and Allan Stanley
Charlie Conacher and Brian Conacher	Muni	Johnny and Ron Wilson
Lionel Conacher and Peter Conacher	Barrie and Dick Meissner and	
Joe, Barry, Ray, and John Cullen	Landon Wilson	COUSINS
Bob Gracie and Graeme Nicolson	Earl Miller and Bill Hay	Bob Attwell and Keith, Bill
Vic and Mark and Marty Howe	Muzz and Lynn Patrick; Craig and	McCreary Jr. and Sr.
Dennis and Brett Hull	Glenn Patrick	Matthew Barnaby and Ray Sheppard
Jacques Lemaire and Manny	Noel and Robert Picard	Jeff Beukeboom and Joe Nieuwendyk
Fernandez	Roger and Robert Picard	Viacheslav and Yuri Butsayev
Blair and Kevin MacDonald	Gordie and David Roberts	Chris Chelios and Nikos Tselios
Jim McFadden and Bill Mikkelson	Leon and Normand Rochefort	Adam and Butch Deadmarsh
Howard and Paul McNamara	Larry, Wayne, and Floyd Hillman	Anders Eldebrink and Robert
Ron Attwell and Bill McCreary Jr.	and Brian Savage	Nordmark

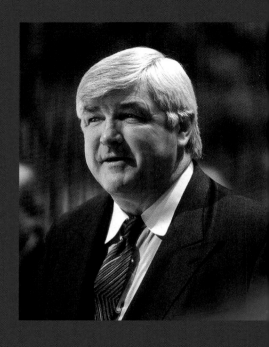

Bob Errey and Ted Lindsay
Ron Francis and Mike Liut
Bernie and Morris Lukowich
Ed Harrison and Ed Sandford
Dale and Paul Hoganson
Tim and Bill Horton
Don Jackson and Brett Hauer
Doug and Wes Jarvis
Dennis Kearns and Shawn Evans
Reg and Alan Kerr
Jerry Korab and Lou Nanne
Guy Leveque and Marty Murray
Barry Melrose and Joey Kocur

Paul and Mark Messier and Joby and
  Mitch Messier
Howie and Brian Morenz
Gus and Keke Mortson
Gerry O'Flaherty and Craig Muni
Barry Pederson and Brian
  Skrudland
Gilbert and Bobby Perreault
Jim Peters Jr. and Glen Currie
Denis and Jean and Marc Potvin
Pat Quinn and Adam Mair
Darcy and Randy Rota
Denis and Jean Savard

Mike Milbury and Dave Silk
Tod Sloan and Dave Keon
Thomas Steen and Dan Labraaten
Bob Sullivan and Wayne Connelly
Joe and Scott Thornton
Keith Tkachuk and Tom Fitzgerald
Perry and Randy Turnbull
Jack and Stephen Valiquette
Ed and Darren Van Impe
Doug and Hayley Wickenheiser

Acknowledgments

My lasting gratitude to Janice Zawerbny for getting this ambitious project off the ground and Michael Mouland at Key Porter for keeping it there. Andrew Murray did a fine job digging up pictures, not only of National Hockey League greats, but also of their lesser-known relatives. Thanks also to Ruta Liormonas at KP.

It was a privilege to work with co-authors Jack Batten, George Johnson, Steve Milton, and Bob Duff, who share a passion for the game and its place in the family. A special thanks to "the Duffer," one of North America's top hockey historians, and Glen R. Goodhand, who both contributed to the list of relatives at the back of the book.

Lance Hornby, Editor
May 2002

Index

Page citations in **boldface** below refer to photographs in the book. Captions for these photographs often contain additional information that is non-boldface in the index, signifying another part of the regular text.